Foods

THAT MAKE

YOU SAY

Mmm-

Published by
JOHN F. BLAIR,
PUBLISHER
1406 Plaza Drive
Winston-Salem, North Carolina 27103
blairpub.com

Library of Congress Cataloging-in-Publication Control Number: 2014019226
ISBN: 978-0-89587-629-4
ISBN: 978-0-89587-630-0 (ebook)

10 9 8 7 6 5 4 3 2 1

Printed in China through Four Colour Print Group,
Louisville, Kentucky

DESIGN BY DEBRA LONG HAMPTON
COVER IMAGE: ©FILE404 / SHUTTERSTOCK

mmm

BY BOB GARNER

CONTENTS

ACKNOWLEDGMENTS

I have had the pleasure of working with Mike Oniffrey in his role as a UNC-TV videographer—"shooter," in our parlance—since 1990. I've always particularly appreciated his high energy and the extra effort he puts into the finer points of lighting non-studio situations. He is also a talented and prolific still photographer who routinely goes above and beyond the requirements of a video shoot by pulling out one or several still cameras and snapping away at practically everyone within range. He is extravagantly generous at sharing these images via email and online, and he always ends up brightening the overall experience for nearly everyone involved with one of our TV projects. Mike took several of the photographs in this book and also shot much of the UNC-TV video footage from which some additional still images were captured. (As a sideline, he is quite adept at creating neckties and other items of clothing, as well as transforming white sneakers into black dress shoes, with the aid of black gaffer's tape.) He has a special touch with creating engaging images of food. I'm glad that readers of this book will be able to enjoy them as much as I have.

Several of the subjects in the book first appeared in different form in my articles in *Our State* magazine. I am indebted to *Our State* for the opportunity to share my passion for traditional North Carolina foods with so many of its readers. What a loyal and approving bunch they are!

I also want to thank UNC-TV once again for putting me in a position to write about food in the first place, and to express my appreciation to David Hardy and Galen Black of the UNC-TV staff for particular help with challenges associated with this book.

My first (and still only) wife, Ruthie, provided invaluable assistance, as she always does. And I thank my terrific children and grandchildren for their constant and refreshing encouragement.

To all the viewers who follow me on my food travels via UNC-TV: getting to meet and chat with you is one of the biggest pleasures of my life. Thanks for watching.

INTRODUCTION

The way in which certain foods become associated with certain regions is an oddity. Since North Carolina is a Southern state, we share a deep devotion to all sorts of commonly enjoyed regional favorites, with the exception of certain barbecue peculiarities found elsewhere south of the Mason-Dixon line. But the allure of certain foods among those favorites attaches itself with particular strength and stubbornness to the consciousness of those from the Old North State.

It certainly has something to do with geography and available food resources. Our long Atlantic coastline, our sounds and estuaries, and our inland rivers have dictated that fish and shellfish be assigned a place near the heart of our foodways. We cherish oyster roasts, digging clams, and our own Outer Banks style of clam chowder. Along some of the rivers flowing into Pamlico and Albemarle sounds, residents have kept alive a tradition revolving around "pine bark" fish stews, or "muddles." Every autumn, coastal insiders begin to look forward to that smoky specialty called charcoal mullet, which celebrates the former prominence of what is now considered a baitfish. And even if we live well removed from the coast, we love fried fish served up in fish camps.

In the third of the state closest to the ocean, the sandy soil lends itself to prolific grape production. Indeed, our coastal plain was home to the first cultivated grapes in America. Our sandy loam is also ideally suited for the cultivation of big, meaty Virginia-type peanuts and perfectly pickle-able cucumbers.

Settlement patterns also had much to do with the history of our favorite foods, and certainly with the emergence of our single most popular food: pork barbecue. The earliest English settlers near the coast found Native Americans barbecuing returned-to-the-wild pigs over pits of glowing hardwood embers—a legacy from the Spanish, who had introduced domesticated swine into the Southeast a hundred years earlier. Today, whole-hog-style is still the signature barbecue presentation of eastern North Carolina. In the Piedmont, on the other hand, later-arriving German settlers imported a preference for the taste of pork shoulder, which is the cut celebrated in the Lexington school of barbecue-ology. Both eastern and Piedmont (Lexington) styles of barbecue are responsible for many spin-off dishes: a bewildering array of barbecue sauces of every description, along with hot sauces and specialty spice sauces; Brunswick stew; hush puppies and corn sticks; and our favorite barbecue desserts, banana pudding and peach cobbler.

The wave of German migration to the North Carolina Piedmont also brought us an enduring fondness for livermush—"the poor man's pâté," a kissing cousin of that Pennsylvania Dutch favorite, scrapple.

Meanwhile, the Moravians, originally from what is now the Czech Republic, kept their area of settlement remarkably compact, centered around present-day Winston-Salem. But the popularity of some of their baked goods, especially Moravian cookies and sugar cake, has become national and even international in scope. Moravian chicken pie, a dish best known more locally, is loved no less than the sweet specialties throughout the north-central Piedmont. And although Krispy Kreme doughnuts had nothing to do with Moravian tradition, these sweet treats sprang from the same Winston-Salem area that brought us warm, gooey sugar cake.

The existence of four well-defined seasons, particularly in the foothills and mountains, is reflected in North Carolina's long love affair with what was originally climate-cured country ham aged over a full year. In our more hurried modern society, the curing process has been "pushed" to keep up with our personal pace, but North Carolinians still love a ham biscuit as much as anyone on the planet.

The hot, muggy climate in much of the state certainly had something to do with the emergence of certain foods and beverages as icons. Not one but three well-known, refreshing soft drinks were either invented or first bottled here: Pepsi-Cola, Cheerwine, and Sun Drop.

In the classic description, North Carolina is a vale of humility between two mountains of conceit—in reference to more aristocratic Virginia and South Carolina. Such a place as North Carolina would figure to be the perfect setting in which equally humble collards could be accorded a place of reverence. Collards were originally considered food for poor people, black and white, not only because they lingered on into the winter, when everything else in the vegetable patch had given up the ghost, but also because they could be made even tastier when seasoned with almost any kind of pork scraps. The strong odor of cooked collards is by itself enough to keep the hardy vegetable out of the kitchens of elite diners, unless they can get someone to cook the collards elsewhere. The same can be said of ramps, or wild leeks, a springtime favorite of many old-time mountain settlers and, nowadays, adventurous festival-going tourists.

And then there are our beloved food peculiarities. Pimento cheese. Fig cake, developed because of the abundance of figs along the coast and, in particular, on Ocracoke Island. Bright Leaf hot dogs, bright red in color and perfectly suited for anointing with mustard, chili, onions, and coleslaw.

In his exhaustive book *Southern Food*, the late John Egerton mused that, "among all classes—those who had plenty and those who had nothing and all the others in between—food was a blessing, a pleasure, a cause for celebration." Nothing could be truer of North Carolina, where the celebratory nature of food and fellowship has never had much to do with the socioeconomic level of our residents. Fact is, the foods that charm us the most have their roots firmly set in non-pretentious soil. It is reflective of our heritage that we probably love them all the more for it.

Although this volume contains recipes for some of the state's traditional favorites, it is more than a cookbook. Readers won't find the standard appetizer–soup–entrée–side dish–dessert organization. Instead, for example, they'll discover banana pudding and peach cobbler grouped closely with barbecue and Brunswick stew, as Tar Heel traditionalists tend to eat them all at the same meal, sometimes even off the same plate. They'll also enjoy photos that seek to do justice to the state's favorites and recommendations for restaurants and festivals where they can indulge in time-tested and praiseworthy versions.

That's as it should be, I hope, as my intention is a kind of cultural tour of North Carolina foodways, progressing from the coast generally, if haphazardly, westward. I hope you enjoy it.

Mmm-mmm . . .

Fish STEW
NOTHING MUCH TO LOOK AT

Eastern North Carolina fish stew is a "guy thing," a dish that's as unpretentious as it gets and that will never win any awards for appetizing appearance. Years ago, I produced a fish stew story for UNC-TV, and the revolted look of the female on-camera host following the last shot—a close-up of the bubbling stew pot—was the exact reaction most male cooks of this unlovely dish hope to provoke.

By longstanding custom, most fish stew is cooked by men, much of it outdoors and nearly all of it outside the civilized confines of a kitchen. The weather must range from cool to downright cold, and the spice level has to range from very warm to downright hot, another point of male pride.

Fish stew is a pot of simmering tomato stock concealing layers of sliced onions, sliced potatoes, and chunks of firm fish on the bone, although the most visible ingredients are the dozen or two poached eggs floating around the top of the bubbling cauldron. The flavor profile is actually fairly mainstream, although the staring egg-eyes and the level of heat make it an acquired taste for most females and, indeed, anyone from outside a four-county area

within a fifty-mile radius of Kinston, on the Neuse River.

To a great many residents of Wayne, Lenoir, Greene, and Pitt counties, though, the cooking of a fish stew is a beloved social occasion, in which the main dish is the centerpiece around which rituals of storytelling, jesting, and not a little social drinking are layered as carefully as the vegetables and fish. While the stew itself is sometimes shaken but never stirred, for fear of breaking the fish into fragments and bones, the details of community life in the vicinity of the Neuse River get a thorough swizzle during the course of a typical fish stew gathering.

The mighty Neuse is the scroll upon which the fish stew story is inscribed. The Neuse, nearly two hundred miles in length, is a diverse ecosystem said to be the largest fish hatchery in the United States. Among the tremendous variety of fish in this enormous natural hatchery is the shad, described by many fishermen as "too bony to eat but great fun to catch." Shad swim up the Neuse and other rivers from the ocean every winter and early spring. They attract not only fishermen, who love the

Opposite: No serving of fish stew is truly complete without eggs, which poach in the stew pot, and a couple of slices of bread for sopping up the flavorful stock.
MIKE ONIFFREY

spirited fight they put up on light and moderate tackle, but also striped bass, or rockfish, which feed on the smaller, bony fish. Stripers, ranging from five to fifteen pounds, are the key ingredient in fish stew. Puppy drum, catfish, or any firm fish—even shad, if one is prepared to put up with the bones—can be substituted, but rockfish is the preferred species.

Not far from Kinston, several past generations of fishermen hauled enormous quantities of stripers and other fish out of the Neuse in seine nets pulled by tractors. The fish, often cleaned right on the riverbank, were cut crosswise through the bone into chunks and were layered with potatoes and onions in large iron wash pots, which were topped off with water, tomato stock, and lots of pepper.

In one particular riverside area known as Pitch Kettle, an important site for harvesting pine turpentine and producing tar for naval stores, fish stew pots were heated by pine wood laden with hardened pitch—"fat lighter"—and pine bark. Hence, one name for the fish concoction was "pine bark stew." When the stew was nearly done, cooks cracked and slid dozens of raw eggs to poach in the tomato stock. An individual bowl of fish stew ladled from one of these pots was expected to contain a fairly even distribution of fish, potatoes, onions, tomato stock, and one or two eggs to "smooth out" the flavor and texture.

A cousin of Neuse River fish stew is prepared occasionally in the fishing and hunting camps along the Roanoke River farther to the north. It's called "rock muddle." While striper, potatoes, and onions are also central ingredients in this offshoot, tomato juice, soup, or paste are not currently added to the water covering the fish and vegetables, although they were in times past. But the biggest difference is that the raw eggs are usually beaten before they're folded vigorously into the muddle, which is further thickened by several cups of crushed saltine crackers. With its pale, watery-scrambled-egg countenance, the northern muddle looks even more unappetizing than Neuse fish stew, if that's possible. Tradition, however, is everything, and both variants have their staunch defenders.

Versions of fish stew probably existed among the earliest Tuscarora, Coree, Secotan, and Neusiok tribes in the Neuse basin. Similar stews were also well documented over a period of two centuries in eastern Virginia and along North Carolina's Outer Banks. In fact, this region is where the word *muddle* originated. According to the late Bill Neal in *Bill Neal's Southern Cooking*, "Muddle is the traditional feast of the region. The simple vegetables—potatoes, onions, tomatoes—in perfect proportion with the freshest fish achieve the satisfaction sought in all good peasant cooking."

Neuse River fish stew is different from some other well-known peasant-style fish stews, including the French bouillabaisse and the Italian cioppino, in that it contains only one type of fish and no bivalves or shellfish, although the flavor of the tomato stock is similar to that of those other, better-known fish stews.

Throughout eastern and northeastern North Carolina, *muddle* became, over time, simply another name for any type of stew.

The dictionary doesn't recognize that usage, instead defining the word as "a mess." That actually isn't a bad description of either Neuse River stew or the rock muddle of the Roanoke region, given the fish bones, bedraggled poached eggs, and generally seedy appearance of the stew. But to the regions' inhabitants, especially males, they are creations of beauty and gastronomic delight.

When the weather turns cold, there seems to rise among men in the fish stew region an overwhelming desire to get their pots over a flame. Nowadays, most fish stews are cooked over gas burners, rather than wood fires. The ritual takes place in backyards and under carports, at hunting and fishing camps, at clubhouses—even at places of business.

LaGrange, not far from Kinston, is considered something of an epicenter for authentic versions of the classic dish. I attended a fish stew gathering at a private home there several years ago, along with a UNC-TV camera crew.

Gerald Holmes and a friend had cooked a ten-gallon pot of fish stew in the garage behind his home, where they could work "out of the wind," which can play havoc with gas burner flames. When we arrived, they were struggling to carry the full pot uphill to Holmes's carport. There, friends and neighbors were setting up fiberglass tables, laying out pans of thin cornbread, and arranging opened cellophane bags of plain white bread. At many fish stews, particularly all-male events, beer and whiskey are the drinks of choice. But this was a more sedate, husband-and-wife affair, so plastic cups of sweet tea were the most ad-venturous beverages in sight, perhaps in part because several people were attending during their work lunch hour.

After a long and fulsome blessing, folks gathered around Holmes, who presided over the pot, ladling stew into their outstretched bowls. (Fish stews are considered low-down affairs, so paper bowls and plastic spoons are the norm, even though a home event like this one occasionally features actual dinnerware and flatware.) Nearly everyone seemed intent on making sure they got at least one egg. Several women asked for "just vegetables, eggs, and broth—no fish, please."

After getting a bowl containing plenty of everything, including fish, I found an empty spot at the table and dug in. With fish stew, one trick is figuring out how to nibble the chunks of fish off the bones without having to expel bones back into the spoon. If the stew has been properly cooked, the fish will still be firm enough to allow this, yet the broth will have worked its way into the flesh to produce an incredible tenderness and moisture level. The potato slices should hold together—not underdone, yet not crumbly. Waxy varieties of potatoes like redskins seem to work best. The crispy, thin cornbread, which had little flour and no sugar, went well with the spicy stew and was something of an unusual touch for these parts.

Fish stews show up in what many would consider odd locations, although LaGrange residents accept them as everyday life. Anyone making a wintertime visit to one of several stores or offices in town, especially on a Friday afternoon, might be asked to step out back to sample a fresh stew cooked up by the employees on the premises. The practice is so common that many LaGrange residents, male and female, carry bowls and spoons in their pickup-truck toolboxes, just in case a fish stew "happens."

Several years back, I attended a fish stew inside an auto repair garage. On a cold, wet Friday, a few men had broken out the pot and burner and cooked up twenty gallons or so of stew just because it was a slow day. I arrived just as the raw eggs were being added. Once they were fully poached—no runny yolks—the final touch was checking the pepper level. "Fish stew's got to be hot," muttered a couple of kibitzers. "If there's a chill in the air, you want it to warm you all the way down." Bottled hot sauce is a popular condiment, as are crushed red pepper flakes.

In one of the oddest dining tableaux I have ever witnessed, some fifty men and women lined up in the garage and ate standing up, using the parallel tracks of the repair lifts, raised to chest level, to rest their full bowls of fish stew. Everyone used folded slices of soft white bread to dip into the tangy broth—and rolled their eyes in appreciation.

"A fish stew can happen anywhere," Gerald Holmes told me at his gathering. "We like to get together and cook at least once a month, especially during cold weather, and this is pretty much what it's always like. Nothing fancy—just family and friends getting together to share something we all grew up with."

AUTHENTIC EASTERN NORTH CAROLINA FISH STEW

THIS RECIPE calls for cooking the potatoes and onions ahead of time, then adding the fish, rather than layering the ingredients.

1 pound bacon, cut into 1-inch pieces
6 potatoes, peeled and sliced
6 onions, sliced ½-inch thick
1 quart tomato juice
½ teaspoon salt
½ teaspoon pepper
½ teaspoon red pepper
3 pounds fish, cut into 1-inch cubes
   (for boneless fish) or in larger
   chunks sliced crosswise through
   the backbone
1 dozen eggs

Fry bacon. Remove bacon and set aside, saving 2 tablespoons bacon grease in pot. Put potatoes and onions in pot and cover with water. Bring to a boil, then let simmer until potatoes are done. Pour in tomato juice and let stew simmer for 5 minutes. Add salt, pepper, and red pepper and stir. Add fish chunks, making sure they are submerged in the liquid. Do not stir stew from this point, so as to avoid breaking up fish. When fish becomes flaky and white, let stew simmer an additional 20 minutes. Break eggs into stew and bring it to a slow simmer again.

The stew is ready after the eggs are completely done, with the yolks cooked firm. Add bacon before serving, if desired.

FEATURE ATTRACTIONS

KING'S RESTAURANT

This extremely popular family restaurant serves a tasty fish stew that's authentic, yet tailored to mainstream tastes. It doesn't have quite as heavy a tomato broth and is a bit less spicy than other fish stews characteristic of the Kinston-LaGrange area. But a little hot sauce added at the table is all that's really needed. Whereas most of the area's fish stews use chunks of fish on the bone, King's version uses boneless fish fillets. Bones ordinarily add flavor to any fish dish, so their absence may lower the richness of the overall taste. Then again, one doesn't have to worry about swallowing any stray bones. The majority of people probably won't miss them.

Most local fish stew cooks begin with rendered bacon fat, in which the onions are sautéed. But many remove the bacon itself before adding the other ingredients. King's version leaves the bacon in. Each bowlful is likely to contain several slices of the crispy pork, definitely a plus for me.

Its location on the main route from the Triangle and Triad to the Crystal Coast has made King's one of the largest restaurants in

King's Restaurant
MIKE ONIFFREY

the South. Seating eight hundred diners, it serves eight thousand pounds of barbecue, six thousand pounds of chicken, and fifteen hundred pounds of collards each month. Frank King opened a country store on the site in 1936. Eventually, he added a poolroom in the back of the store. The genesis of the restaurant came when King began heating canned food from the store on a stove so hungry pool players wouldn't have to leave the tables. The place became quite a teenage hangout during the 1950s. One of the area's most noted lovers' lanes was reportedly located behind an enormous billboard in King's back parking lot.

King's is a cheerful restaurant specializing in a consistent menu of comfort foods. Booths and tables in the main Bright Leaf dining room are set with red-checkered cloths, and the somewhat dark interior is brightened by neon signs, including those advertising several brands of beer, even though the restaurant doesn't serve beer. You'll find the service friendly and fast.

Fish stew is a specialty during the fall, winter, and early-spring months. Call ahead to make sure it is being served.

KING'S RESTAURANT

405 East New Bern Road (U.S. 70)

Kinston, N.C. 28501

252-527-2101

www.kingsbbq.com

Lunch and dinner, Monday through Friday; breakfast, lunch, and dinner, Saturday and Sunday

KEN'S GRILL

This is no doubt the best-known little place for fish stew in eastern North Carolina, at least in a restaurant setting. Ken and David Eason run a simple, box-like restaurant alongside U.S. 70 between Goldsboro and Kinston, a few miles east of the exit for LaGrange. The place stays jammed most of the time, especially on Friday, which is the only day of the week fish stew is served. It used to be a fall- and winter-only specialty at Ken's but is now served year-round.

For nearly twenty-five years, the restaurant has been offering an outstanding version of the area's iconic stew, probably due to the fact that Ken is quite the fisherman and knows a lot about the history of fishing and riverbank stew making in the vicinity. His father-in-law, Jimmy Jones, shares Ken's love of fishing and cooking. He's the one who persuaded Ken to add fish stew to the menu at his grill. It seems Jones once ran a fish market. And like many businesses in the LaGrange area, his place used to feature house-made fish stew. "I always thought fish stew would go over well out here on the highway at Ken's, given the visibility of the place," says Jones.

The fish stew at Ken's is so popular that the original production of a couple of five-gallon pots per week has quintupled to nearly ten pots per week today. Another specialty, fried fish, is also served only on Friday.

This stew is just about perfectly balanced—not too spicy-hot, not too thick with tomato sauce, chunks of rockfish that stay on

Ken's Grill
MIKE ONIFFREY

the bone and don't flake off into pieces, plenty of potatoes and savory poached eggs.

Ken's is also known for serving some of eastern North Carolina's most perfectly seasoned barbecue on Wednesday and Saturday year-round and incredibly messy but delicious hand-pattied burgers (complete with homemade chili) every day it's open. Despite its location beside a busy highway rather than in a downtown setting, this eatery is one of the best examples of a simple restaurant becoming a community gathering spot and "public house" that I have visited anywhere in North Carolina.

KEN'S GRILL

7645 U.S. 70

LaGrange, N.C. 28551

252-566-4765

Breakfast, lunch, and dinner, Wednesday through Saturday

GRIFTON SHAD FESTIVAL

The best way to experience fish stew is to attend a private event. But if you don't have a contact for such an invitation, the annual Grifton Shad Festival in April provides a great opportunity to sample this regional specialty.

The Grifton Lions Club prepares and serves the stew—outdoors, as is proper. Shad aren't actually used in the stew (although they once were) because they contain too many bones, which has led some to say the fish are "more fun to catch than to eat." So why was the festival named for the humble shad? Organizers respond, with perfect logic, "Well, they don't eat azaleas at the Azalea Festival, nor do they eat mules at Mule Days." Striped bass—or rockfish—are sometimes difficult to obtain in the quantities needed for the Shad Festival, so Grifton's version of the stew is made with locally raised catfish, an excellent substitute.

The festival is a fairly typical large street fair named for the fish that swim upstream to spawn in Contentnea Creek, a Neuse River tributary that flows through Grifton. The town is located northeast of Kinston near the legendary fish stew cooking spot known as Pitch Kettle, so the tradition is strongly rooted in the community.

GRIFTON SHAD FESTIVAL

P.O. Box 147

Grifton, N.C. 28530

252-524-4356

griftonshadfestival.com

CHARCOAL MULLET
AN INSIDER'S TREAT

THESE DAYS, mullet is often thought of as a baitfish. Refrigeration has vastly increased the variety of fish available to consumers, and flounder, red drum, mahi-mahi, sea trout, grouper, and tuna have become North Carolina's coastal dining favorites, at least among seasonal visitors.

But many longtime coastal residents still cherish the smoky autumn treat they call "charcoal mullet"—unscaled mullet fillets cooked skin side down on a grill over glowing embers. (Before charcoal grills became popular after World War II, whole mullet were skewered lengthwise on sticks. With one end of the sticks stuck into the ground, the mullet were arranged teepee fashion around a bed of wood coals.)

Mullet—known variously as striped mullet, gray mullet, and jumping mullet—have a full, meaty flavor that some call "nutty." During the 1800s and early 1900s, they were abundant and popular along the North Carolina coast. Cold fronts and northeast winds during the fall triggered massive mullet migrations southward along the Atlantic coast. In fact, these weather patterns were referred to as "mullet blows." Part-time fishermen flocked to the coast and set up seaside camps, from which they netted hundreds, even thousands, of barrels of mullet, which were preserved by heavy salting before refrigeration became universal. (Today, one of the last haul-seine operations in the country involves mullet fishermen along Carteret County's Bogue Banks in late fall. Dories are used to set the nets, which, when full of fish, are pulled to shore by tractors.)

Before charcoal grills came into vogue, mullet were commonly skewered on sticks and cooked over an open fire.
UNC-TV

Much of the mullet harvest was shipped out of state, but many North Carolinians were customers as well. The railroad between Morehead City and Goldsboro, built in 1858, carried such a quantity of the fish that it was nicknamed "the Mullet Line." Many fishing families along the coast and on the Outer Banks actually sustained life on fish like spot and mullet. The mullet's roe and gizzards were also highly valued. But over time, diners began bypassing mullet for the other varieties of fish that began showing up regularly in seafood markets. With its visible layer of white fat, the mullet began to be regarded as too oily, too pungent, and too . . . well, humble for refined palates.

Mullet can be stewed or pan-fried, but most old coastal salts prefer charcoal-grilling. The fish must be filleted but not scaled. It should be lightly seasoned with salt and pepper or a favorite blend such as Cajun seasoning and grilled mostly scale side down over a moderate fire, just long enough to cook the fish's flesh without drying it out. The skin and scales actually serve as a pan in which the fish cooks, moistened with—and in effect frying in—its own abundant fat, which creates aromatic smoke and steam as it drips onto the coals. The charred skin and scales also serve as a plate from which the smoky-tasting fish is forked up before the blackened exterior is discarded.

Liz Biro is a freelance food writer, food blogger, and restaurant guide from Onslow County who has written about charcoal mullet for years. On the next page is her recipe, which appeared in the *Wilmington Star-News* in 2007.

CHARCOAL MULLET

2 pounds striped mullet fillets, skin
    and scales intact
salt and pepper to taste
¼ cup Carolina Treet Cooking
    Barbecue Sauce, ½ cup bottled
    Italian dressing, or a seasoning
    blend of garlic powder, paprika,
    Texas Pete, and butter to taste
    (optional)

Prepare a medium-hot charcoal fire in a grill or set a gas grill on medium-high or high. Rinse fillets, pat dry, and season with salt and pepper.

If using Carolina Treet, brush a light coating of sauce on flesh side of fillets.

If using Italian dressing, pour over fish and let marinate in the refrigerator for 20 to 30 minutes.

If using seasoning blend, sprinkle a light coating of garlic powder, paprika, and Texas Pete on flesh side of fillets and lightly dot with butter.

Place plain or seasoned fillets in a single layer on the grate, skin side down, and close the grill's lid. Cook for 8 to 10 minutes, depending on thickness of fillets. The flesh will flake easily and release from the skin when the fish is cooked. Slide a spatula between the grill and the fish, lifting skin and all onto a serving plate. Serves 3 to 4.

NOTE: Carolina Treet and Texas Pete are featured in the Sauces chapter (see pages 167-70).

The blackened scales and skin of grilled charcoal mullet serve as both the cooking pan, in which the fish "fries" in its own fat, and the disposable plate from which the firm, pungent flesh is eaten.
UNC-TV

You Say FISH CAMP I SAY Fish House

In some parts of the country, especially the upper Midwest, the term *fish camp* might bring to mind the image of an unassuming lakeside resort, the kind of place with a main building, scattered rustic cabins, and some boat docks. It would be a destination for catching fish, maybe with the help of a local guide.

However, in the North Carolina Piedmont and upland South Carolina, a fish camp is simply a family-friendly seafood restaurant serving fresh and saltwater fish, mostly deep-fried, at reasonable prices. The last criterion is important, because fish camps attract a largely working-class clientele. They have always been popular in the textile mill belt as restaurants where good, simple food can be enjoyed on a budget.

Nearer the coastal areas of the Carolinas, fish camps are more often referred to as *Calabash-style* seafood houses, named for the tiny Brunswick County town just north of the South Carolina border. They're really the same thing, except that fish camps are slightly more likely to serve catfish along with their saltwater choices, and their portions may be a little larger (and the prices lower) than at Calabash-style houses.

Stephen Criswell is a native of Gaston County, which still has at least a dozen fish camps, even though some legendary local places have closed. He says fish camps "still draw loyal crowds on Thursday, Friday, and Saturday nights, who line up for half and whole orders of some of the best seafood around."

Criswell is a food historian, as well as being an English professor at the University of South Carolina–Lancaster. He's written definitively on hush puppies and fish camps for the *New Encyclopedia of Southern Culture*, among other publications.

Says Criswell, "Fish camps are hardly dives, but most proprietors eschew table linens and china for a comfortable décor, where fried seafood and sides of fries, hushpuppies, and coleslaw are served to jean- and T-shirt-clad patrons in ladder-back chairs at uncovered wooden tables, surrounded by paneled walls decorated with stuffed fish or signs warning against swearing, drinking, and fighting on the premises."

What later became permanent restaurants

started out in many cases as simple day camps on the banks of Piedmont rivers. Textile-mill workers enjoyed fishing on their days off and discovered that river catfish—like most fish—taste better when they're cleaned and fried right on the spot, especially if they're lightly coated with cornmeal or flour.

The owners of these "campsites" often set up semi-permanent sheds on the riverbank and had their employees heat up pans of lard. For a small fee, they would fry up an angler's catch right there. This is similar to the way some famous coastal seafood restaurants got started. The owner of a large boat might take customers offshore for some fishing, then bring them back to the dock, where a partner would cook the fishermen's catch on a kerosene stove in some unprepossessing shack outfitted with trestle tables.

According to fish camp chronicler Criswell, one of the first of the Piedmont riverbank camps was in Gaston County, where a local textile worker named Luther Lineburger started cooking fish beside the Catawba River in the 1930s. Over time, Lineburger saw the potential profit in turning a rough fishing hangout into a family-friendly, alcohol-free restaurant. By the late 1940s, he built a dining-hall-style place on the original site. It eventually grew to seat five hundred persons. Three generations of his family members operated Lineburger's Fish Fry until it finally shut down in the 1990s. Dozens of other fish camps followed, many of them closely held family affairs. They evolved into not-at-all-fancy fish restaurants serving mostly coastal seafood, rather than fish pulled out of the river. At one time, Gaston County alone had some forty fish camps.

Southern folk wisdom has always maintained that fish should be fried outdoors. It wasn't primarily a concern about fishy odors that spawned the conviction, but rather some magic in the very words *fish fry*. No one has trouble visualizing a freshly caught mountain trout sizzling in a cast-iron frying pan set up on a grate over a flickering campfire. The arresting aroma of breaded fish bubbling and gurgling away in hot, fragrant oil mingles as well with the salt tang of ocean air as it does with the evening scents of inland river mud. This effect is best achieved by cooking where you catch, or at least outside the house.

Oh, but there's that other possibility. You can forget the fuss of cooking altogether, get cleaned up, and simply show up somewhere where friendly waitresses who call you "sugar" will make it all appear before you like magic. At the shore, on the riverbank, or in a humble fish camp, fried fish is food for the common man.

At fish houses near the coast, oysters, shrimp, scallops, deviled crab, soft-shell crab, and even some local croaker, mullet, and other panfish appear on the menu more often than is the case at many Piedmont and mountain fish camps. At Calabash-style fish places, catfish is generally featured less often.

North Carolina's seafood tastes have become more sophisticated. Plenty of grilled, broiled, baked, baked-and-stuffed, blackened, stewed, poached, and parchment-wrapped fish and shellfish are served these days. We're all trying not only to eat healthier

Even inland fish camps now serve mostly saltwater fish, along with farm-raised catfish.
UNC-TV

but also to explore richer and deeper seafood flavors and presentations.

But go to a fish house where the parking lot is full to overflowing on a Wednesday to Saturday night. There, you'll find that nine out of ten of the plain-folk diners are getting in touch with their heritage by enjoying fried fish with all the trimmings.

In terms of general family dining outside the home, flounder seems to be North Carolina's favorite fried fish in all regions. In the mountains, fresh rainbow trout might have an edge. And catfish—once consigned by polite society to consumption by backwoodsmen—is now making its way onto a great many tables in North Carolina and elsewhere in the Southeast.

Below are tips on preparing North Carolina's favorite fried fish.

TROUT

Though only the brook trout is native to North Carolina, brown and rainbow trout can also now be found in our mountain streams, thanks to fish hatcheries.

The rainbow trout, a cousin to the salmon, is, like that fish, native to the streams flowing into the Pacific. It was introduced to western North Carolina waterways in the late 1800s. Plenty of fishermen find the rainbow a hard-fighting species that's great fun to catch. But

Farm-raised North Carolina rainbow trout cooks up so beautifully that it is even featured at coastal restaurants like Blue Point in the Outer Banks community of Duck.

virtually all rainbow trout for consumption are raised in commercial fish farms and fish-for-a-fee small ponds, most of them concentrated near the Great Smoky Mountains. Transylvania County has more for-real rainbow trout farms, as opposed to ponds, than any other county, followed by Graham and Macon. For over a hundred years, rainbow trout have been featured on many restaurant and inn dining tables. Without question, they're the region's favorite fish, especially when it comes to eating places that are a step or two above fish camps in price and ambiance.

There is hardly a way to cook a rainbow trout—baked, broiled, pecan- or quinoa-encrusted, poached—that isn't delicious. When it comes to frying, the choices are pan-fried or deep-fried. The former requires a relatively small amount of butter or oil, while the fish is submerged in oil in the latter process. Pan-frying is not only more practical for home cooking but also suits itself better to the texture and flavor of this particular fish, in my opinion.

Whole rainbows shouldn't be scaled before cooking. A thin coat of a natural jelly-like substance permeates the scales and holds breading without the fish having to be dipped in liquid before being dredged. You should remove the gills, but you can leave the head and tail on the fish while you cook it, if you like. The blood line should also be scraped off the backbone before you bread and fry the trout.

To pan-fry a whole trout or trout fillets, first rinse the fish and pat it dry with a paper towel, since this helps make the skin crisper. Give it a light coating of self-rising flour (which already contains salt) and pepper, shaking off any excess flour. You might prefer to pan-fry the trout with no breading at all, as that will get you a little closer to the fish's subtle flavor.

Butter is a great choice for pan-frying. You can use as little as two or as many as four tablespoons of butter to cook a couple of one-pound trout. Heat the butter over moderate heat until it's bubbling (but not turning brown or smoking), then fry the fish for about five minutes on each side. The internal temperature should be around 145 degrees. The attractive pink flesh should flake easily with a fork and shouldn't look the slightest bit translucent or transparent. But you don't want to overcook it either, since this will make it tough and dry. A slice of lemon and a sprig of parsley will garnish the beautiful golden brown fish admirably.

Rainbow trout are gorgeous. Yes, poor mountain folk have long caught them using homemade fishing poles and dough balls for bait, but the species nevertheless has an elegant aura, bringing to mind the image of the well-dressed and well-equipped fly-fisherman.

CATFISH

The catfish, by comparison, has always been thought of as a cheap food source, something only a poor man would eat. Catfish have long, evil-looking whiskers and slimy skin with no scales. River or "mud" cats are often caught on trotlines baited with chicken livers or other such unappetizing scraps. Many refined Southerners, and certainly the females of that species, have been known to sniff, "I don't eat catfish."

Today's farm-raised catfish thrive, however, on an all-grain diet. They have a mild, sweet flavor, no fishy smell, and a delicate texture that seems totally at odds with their rascally appearance. As a matter of fact, catfish often need to be cooked a bit longer than most other types of fish so the flesh will firm up enough to have a satisfying "bite" to it. Otherwise, it can be said with some truth that "there's no *there* there." Catfish are clearly growing in popularity, especially in the southeastern states. More catfish are farm-produced in the United States each year than all other species of farmed fish put together.

Both skinned whole fish and catfish fillets can be found in many grocery stores, along with catfish "nuggets," which are basically hunks of fillet that didn't come off the bone just right but that eat just as nicely as whole fillets, if you aren't trying to impress with appearance. Normally, I prefer fish on the bone, but in the case of catfish, having the bones in place seems to slow the interior cooking too much; the interior flesh never seems to get

Pan-fried catfish with creole mayonnaise, served at Lucky 32 restaurant in Greensboro
MIKE ONIFFREY

done enough to satisfy me before the outside becomes overcooked.

Catfish simply begs to be deep-fried. The secret is to quickly seal in the moisture and flavor by dropping the fillets into oil that is at exactly the right temperature, 350 degrees, and letting them cook for about five minutes until they're the right shade of golden brown. Now, don't worry if you don't have a deep fryer or deep-fry thermometer, since the average catfish cook over the generations has never owned those items. You'll have enough oil if you fill an average-sized cast-iron frying pan about half full—about an inch and a half of oil—and heat it until the oil appears to "wiggle." You can use canola or some other oil if you like, but for frying fish, I prefer corn oil.

I like to salt catfish fairly heavily and let it sit until it's close to room temperature before frying it. Since the idea is for it to cook suf-ficiently in the center before the outside gets too brown, I don't want the center to be too cool when I begin.

Many cooks like to dip catfish either in milk, a beaten-eggs-and-milk mixture, or buttermilk before dredging the whole fish or fillets in yellow cornmeal. For the popular variation called "salt and pepper catfish," add one teaspoon of salt and a couple tablespoons of freshly ground pepper to each cup of cornmeal. That's in addition to whatever salt and pepper you sprinkle on the fish itself.

Other folks like to dip the whole fish or fillets into a batter comprised of one-third cup of cornmeal, a quarter-cup of flour, half a diced onion, and enough beer to make the batter thin. (If you leave the batter too thick, it will soak up more oil than you want.) In this method, the fillets will look almost like they're boiling in the hot oil. Once they reach the proper temperature, drain them on folded paper towels or, more authentically, folded brown paper bags.

FLOUNDER

The efficient distribution of saltwater fish and shellfish has totally changed the menu of fish camps in the North Carolina Piedmont and mountains. That has led flounder to become the state's most popular fried fish, even far inland from its native waters. Flounder has a mild, non-threatening flavor, leading a lot of people, including many who don't love most fish, to order it more or less by default when they make their weekly or bi-weekly visits to their favorite fish camp.

Both pan-frying and deep-frying suit flounder to a *T*. Most fish houses prefer to work with flounder fillets, but quite a few cooks like to fry small flounder whole, since the bones are large and not at all troublesome and since they add flavor to the fish.

To pan-fry flounder fillets, rinse and dry them with paper towels, then coat them with a light covering of all-purpose flour, salt, and pepper. Cook them in just a couple tablespoons of oil over moderate heat for four or five minutes on each side until the flesh is flaky. This is a welcome change for people

Flounder Night is a popular weekly event at Pam's Farmhouse restaurant in Raleigh.
MIKE ONIFFREY

who have had only deep-fried flounder in the past. The texture is lighter and the flavor more up-front.

For deep-frying, many cooks soak flounder fillets in milk for fifteen minutes, then coat them with a mixture consisting of half cornmeal and half pancake mix, plus salt and pepper to taste. Commercial seafood breading mixes also work well with flounder. The fillets are deep-fried in the same manner I described for catfish, with no special equipment needed. By the way, a tip for gauging the temperature of hot oil, if you don't have a proper thermometer, is that a one-inch cube of bread should take one minute to fry to a perfect golden brown. That result will put you very close to 350 degrees.

FEATURE ATTRACTIONS

SANITARY FISH MARKET AND RESTAURANT

Morehead City, on the Crystal Coast, is home to undoubtedly the most storied seafood restaurant in North Carolina, the Sanitary Fish Market and Restaurant, which celebrated its seventy-fifth anniversary in February 2013.

For several generations of North Carolinians, dining at the Sanitary has been part of the rhythm of life, a periodic family ritual. The Sanitary was once considered among the top ten seafood restaurants in the country, so well known that a postcard from London addressed simply, "Sanitary Fish Market, USA," reached its destination.

The place had a humble beginning. Cofounder Tony Seamon had a charter boat, grandiosely called a yacht by some, with overnight accommodations for eight. "Captain Tony" often cooked fresh-caught seafood for his guests right on the boat. His friend Ted Garner (a relative of mine, by the way) operated a little seafood market on the Morehead City waterfront and used to help drum up charter business for Seamon. Folks told the two they should open a restaurant, and in 1938, they did just that, in a compact, humble store building. The Sanitary moved to larger quarters slightly east of its original location after World War II and has expanded several times at that site. The Garner family now owns the enterprise.

The exploding popularity of the Beaufort–Morehead City–Atlantic Beach–Emerald Isle area brought increased competition and new challenges. While the area has many more restaurants now, tightened fishing regulations mean fewer suppliers, which dictates that Jeff Garner, the cofounder's grandson, must often go as far as Ocracoke or Oregon Inlet to find fresh seafood. Garner also fishes offshore for tuna, dolphin, and wahoo on the restaurant's own boat, which runs on biofuel refined from the Sanitary's used cooking oil.

The restaurant boasts an outside deck, a large, new dock for boating customers, and occasional live entertainment. A bar was added in 2012—an ironic twist for a restaurant

Morehead City's Sanitary Fish Market and Restaurant opened in this building, just west of its present location, in 1938.
SANITARY FISH MARKET AND RESTAURANT

where one of the most memorable features is the historic sign, still on display, warning against drunkenness.

SANITARY FISH MARKET AND RESTAURANT

501 Evans Street

Morehead City, N.C. 28557

252-247-3111

www.sanitaryfishmarket.com

Lunch and dinner daily; call for off-season schedule

SALTBOX SEAFOOD JOINT

Saveur magazine called this takeout-only place a "tiny but mighty seafood shack." It's the brainchild of chef Ricky Moore, a New Bern native who trained at the Culinary Institute of America. Moore firmly believes outstanding food "can happen anywhere." It certainly happens here, in what many would consider an unlikely location: a one-room, walk-up eatery on the northern edge of downtown Durham.

Around half the menu, which changes

Saltbox Seafood Joint
UNC-TV

often according to what's fresh, is offered in the form of seafood rolls, all of which feature your choice of fish or shellfish, sub rolls toasted with shrimp-infused butter, and a topping of Moore's lemony coleslaw, which contains coconut but no mayonnaise. The plates are beautiful, plenteous servings of fried, blackened, or grilled seafood, some showcasing small fish cooked whole and bone-in for extra flavor and moisture.

Fine touches abound. The thin-sliced, twice-fried potatoes, shaped like potato chips, are nicely flavored with attractive bits of sautéed onion and green pepper. There are crunchy, fried Brussels sprouts. The tartar sauce is homemade and unique, not at all like the sweet-pickle-based version on most restaurant tables. Moore creates and mixes his own spice blends and fusses over each plate,

sprinkling and plumping and arranging to a fare-thee-well. Off to the side sits a pot of aromatic, creamy grits simmered in crab-steeped milk, which Moore serves topped with rich, luscious lump crabmeat. The homemade iced tea and lemon punch are exceptional.

Don't let the modest appearance of this quirky seafood shed fool you. No matter what you order, it will be memorable. It's a bit on the expensive side but well worth it.

SALTBOX SEAFOOD JOINT

608 North Mangum Street
Durham, N.C. 27701
919-908-8970
www.saltboxseafoodjoint.com
Lunch and dinner, Tuesday through Saturday

LOVE'S FISH BOX

Most fish camps in the Gastonia–Kings Mountain area were built to hold crowds. Love's Fish Box, aptly reflecting its name, is smaller. It has a dining room but no table service. Whether you're there to dine in or get takeout, you place your order at the front counter. Those eating on the spot simply take their plates to the adjoining dining room, help themselves to tableware and napkins, and tuck into their meals.

Love's is best known for its catfish, especially the salt-and-pepper version, but the flounder and perch are top sellers as well, along with shrimp, scallops, oysters, and deviled crab.

Love's Fish Box bustles despite its size. Customers who aren't sure what they want to order will get lots of suggestions and attention from the friendly counter staff, so not having table service is really no drawback.

LOVE'S FISH BOX

1104 Shelby Road

Kings Mountain, N.C. 28086

704-739-4036

lovesfishbox.com

Lunch and dinner, Tuesday through Saturday

Love's Fish Box
MIKE ONIFFREY

CALABASH SEAFOOD HUT/COLEMAN'S

Coleman's is on the Calabash waterfront, while the Calabash Seafood Hut is on the road leading to it. Both restaurants are owned by Joanne Coleman, the widow of founder Virgil "Tinky" Coleman, who was a longtime boat captain as well as a restaurateur.

The Seafood Hut, the smaller of the two places, has only around fifteen tables, so the cooking is done in small batches, which is almost always a good thing. There are no heat lamps, so everything comes pretty much right out of the lard (yes, lard) and goes directly to the tables. True to the Calabash tradition, the seafood is moistened in evaporated milk and lightly coated with self-rising flour. The hush puppies aren't overly sweet, and the coleslaw has next to no mayonnaise; its dressing is mainly a sweetened vinegar. If you have a half-hour or so to spare, the Seafood Hut is probably the most personable seafood spot in Calabash.

CALABASH SEAFOOD HUT

1125 River Road

Calabash, N.C. 28467

910-579-6723

Lunch and dinner, Tuesday through Sunday

Calabash Seafood Hut

COLEMAN'S ORIGINAL CALABASH SEAFOOD RESTAURANT

9931 Nance Street

Calabash, N.C. 28467

910-579-6875

RED STAG GRILL

This hunting-lodge-themed restaurant in Biltmore Village's Grand Bohemian Hotel in Asheville features farm-raised trout from Sunburst Trout Farms in nearby Canton, which supplies many of the best restaurants and upscale groceries in North Carolina and neighboring states. The fare here doesn't come cheap, but the restaurant's fans say the fish is cooked to perfection and that the overall ambiance of the place is worth the occasional splurge.

RED STAG GRILL

Grand Bohemian Hotel

11 Boston Way

Asheville, N.C. 28803

828-398-5600

www.bohemianhotelasheville.com

Breakfast, lunch, and dinner daily

The chef adds sauce to a trout dish at Red Stag Grill.
GRAND BOHEMIAN HOTEL

Fish House Restaurant

FISH HOUSE RESTAURANT

The Fish House serves old-fashioned fried seafood in an upscale setting. Other preparation styles are available as well. The restaurant has an active bar scene.

FISH HOUSE RESTAURANT
Blue Water Point Marina
West Beach Drive at Fifty-seventh Place
Oak Island, N.C. 28465
910-278-6092
www.bluewaterpointmotel.com
Lunch on Saturday and Sunday; dinner daily

CYPRESS GRILL

This place, the last of the old-time herring shacks on the banks of the Roanoke River, opens only during the herring run from January to April. It also offers a wide variety of other fried fish and shellfish, plus famous homemade pies.

CYPRESS GRILL
1520 Steward Street
Jamesville, N.C. 27846
252-792-4175
Call for dates and hours

Fried herring at the Cypress Grill, which is open only during the herring run from January to April

Holland's Shelter Creek Fish Camp

HOLLAND'S SHELTER CREEK FISH CAMP

This is a rustic creek-side restaurant featuring down-home fried seafood, frog legs, catfish stew, and a Cajun-spiced fish plate, along with general-store merchandise and hand-scooped ice-cream cones at the front counter.

HOLLAND'S SHELTER CREEK FISH CAMP

8315 N.C. 53 East

Burgaw, N.C. 28425

910-259-3399

Lunch and dinner, Monday through Saturday

ATKINSON MILLING

There has been a mill at the Atkinson site in Johnston County since 1757.
ATKINSON MILLING

IF YOU DINE IN restaurants across a ten-county area of eastern and central North Carolina, chances are you've enjoyed cornmeal products and bread mixes from Atkinson in Johnston County, a milling company that has been in business since before the American Revolution. Although the bulk of Atkinson's business is institutional, a great many individual customers also purchase the company's stone-ground cornmeal, hush puppy mix, biscuit mix, pancake mix, stone-ground grits, and breading mixes for seafood and chicken. Atkinson products are available online and are carried by numerous specialty stores, including several at the State Farmers' Market

in Raleigh. The crispy, baked-then-fried cornbread sticks familiar to regulars at seafood and barbecue restaurants around Wilson and Rocky Mount also come from Atkinson.

The original mill at the site on the Little River was built in April 1757. The property was owned by succeeding generations of the Richardson family until ownership passed by marriage to the Atkinson family in 1859 and to the McLean family in 1950. After rebuilding the mill in 1951, one year after it was totally destroyed by fire, the McLeans sold the property to Ray and Betty Wheeler in 1971. The Wheelers had been employed by the mill and had been responsible for its operation for thirteen years before they assumed ownership. Their children and grandchildren are now taking over.

Grist milling is an ancient method of grinding grain between two stones to produce bread. In biblical days, people placed wheat or barley on one stone and rubbed the grain with another stone to grind it. The same essential process is used at Atkinson Milling today to grind cornmeal. The stones are larger, of course, and more power is needed to turn them. As has been the case since the mill's founding, much of the grinding is still done with water power from the dammed Little River.

At the time the current mill structure was rebuilt in the early 1950s, Johnston and surrounding counties each had from twenty to forty gristmills. Today, Atkinson is the only remaining water-powered gristmill operating in Johnston County, while neighboring Wake, Wilson, and Wayne counties have none at all.

Farmers truck corn to the mill, where the grain is cleaned at least three times until nothing is left but kernels suitable for grinding. The ground meal is never touched by human hands, but is rather moved by air from one processing location to another, then bagged by semi-automatic machinery.

Ray Wheeler says, "We specialize in grinding our meal fine, as opposed to the roller-ground meal you usually find in the grocery stores. It's a slow process, but it's worth it."

ATKINSON MILLING COMPANY

95 Atkinson Mill Road (intersection of N.C. 42 and N.C. 39)

Selma, N.C. 27576

800-948-5707 or 919-965-3547

www.atkinsonmilling.com

DOWN EAST LEMON MILK PIE

THIS PIE IS ALSO known as Harkers Island Lemon Milk Pie or Atlantic Beach Pie. Particularly in Carteret County, it is considered one of the most traditional desserts to enjoy after a meal of fish or other seafood. Some old-timers used to believe that eating dessert after a seafood meal would make you sick—unless the dessert was the type of lemon pie served in restaurants along the Morehead City waterfront.

DOWN EAST LEMON MILK PIE

CRUST
½ cup butter
1½ sleeves Ritz crackers (some
   people use saltines)

FILLING
14-ounce can Eagle Brand sweetened condensed milk
3 egg yolks
6 tablespoons fresh-squeezed
   lemon juice

MERINGUE
4 egg whites
1 teaspoon vanilla flavoring
6 tablespoons sugar

Melt butter and crush crackers. Mix to-gether butter and crackers, then press mixture firmly on to bottom and sides of a pie pan. Set aside. (Some recipes call for baking the crust for 10 to 15 minutes, although it really isn't necessary.)

Combine sweetened condensed milk, egg yolks, and lemon juice in a mixing bowl. Whip with a hand whisk until ingredients are well combined and yolks are fully incorporated. Pour filling into the prepared pie shell.

Using an electric mixer, whip egg whites in a mixing bowl. Add vanilla while whipping. Slowly add 1 tablespoon of sugar at a time as you continue to beat egg whites. After all the sugar has been added, continue whipping until peaks form. Top pie with meringue and swirl into a decorative pattern with a knife or spatula.

Bake at 350 degrees for about 10 minutes, watching to see that meringue becomes lightly browned but not burned. Remove from oven and let cool for 1 hour, then refrigerate.

Crassotrea Virginica,
THE DIVINE ATLANTIC OYSTER

Steaming, roasting, and eating Newport River oysters are some of my most vivid recollections of my childhood in the 1950s.

It wasn't something that happened often. Although both my parents grew up on farms outside Newport and I was born nearby, my father's career as a navy pilot kept us moving around frequently. I never actually lived in the then-tiny Carteret County community. But we made frequent trips to Newport to visit both sets of grandparents. During the fall, winter, and early spring, feasting on oysters was often part of the homecoming ritual.

One of my clearest recollections is of my father and paternal grandfather dumping hosed-off oysters from a bushel basket into my grandmother's kitchen sink. Rather than steam the oysters outside, they would pour a couple of large pots of boiling water over the bivalves in the sink and cover them with kitchen towels. While they waited five minutes or so for the oysters to heat up (this method produced only a light steaming), they would consume a couple dozen raw oysters. No fancy spread of melted butter, hot sauce,

or horseradish, but rather saltine crackers and a Mason jar of long, thin hot-pepper pods in briny vinegar. Period. Salt and pepper were never brought out, since the oysters were already salty-tasting.

I can also clearly picture several front-yard oyster roasts at the home of my father's father. (In Newport, at least in those days, people used their backyards for planting vegetable gardens and cultivating fig trees.) Four cinder blocks would be arranged on end in a rectangle, and a wood fire would be built in the middle. When the fire was going strong, an old Dr Pepper sign or some other suitable piece of sheet metal would be balanced on the upturned cinder blocks so it was centered over the flames and coals. Three or four shovelfuls of oysters would be spread evenly on the sheet metal, and then several layers of soaked burlap bags would be laid over the pile to create steam. The steamed oysters would be dumped out on an old dinette table covered with newspaper. Men would stand around and open the oysters, maybe eating them directly from the shells, or perhaps dunking them in bowls of pepper vinegar and plopping them on crackers. Women stayed in the house or sat in the front-porch swing, seldom venturing out to sample the oysters. We had no cornbread or coleslaw, no Down East lemon milk pie, and no other festive touches. None were needed.

I never really got the hang of opening oysters until years later, so the only ones I ate were those my father opened and passed to me on crackers. But since he was pretty thoughtful about doing that, I made out okay. I remember that those oysters were always plump and firm and meaty. Even as a kid, I loved them.

My dad always told "the Oyster Joke" at those gatherings: "Fellow comes along with a big ol' oyster on the half shell and says to another fellow, 'Hey, I'll bet you a dollar you can't swallow this oyster.' Other fellow grabs the shell and slurps down the oyster with one chug. Says, 'Hand over the dollar.' First fellow looks puzzled and says, 'Well, I'll be doggoned. Six other men have tried to swallow that same oyster, and you're the first one to keep it down.' Second fellow gags and throws up the oyster. First fellow picks it up off the ground, puts it back on the shell, collects his dollar, and walks away whistling."

What fascinated me most at those oyster roasts was the galvanized washtub full of ice-cold soft drinks. My father and grandfather would have picked up a half-block of ice at the Newport icehouse, then reduced it inside the tub to fist-sized chunks with the aid of a couple of ice picks. The "Co-Colas," Pepsis, Dr Peppers, TruAdes, and Nehis cooling under that cascade of melting ice were the most lovely, colorful assortment of refresh-

ments I had ever seen, and reaching into that tub of icy water would numb my arm to the elbow for ten minutes. Having previously demonstrated that, left to my own devices, I would make myself nauseated by guzzling a half-dozen bottles (I normally was allowed bottled drinks only as a special treat, and only in Newport), I was required to ask an adult to use the metal church-key opener to pry open an icy bottle for me. Most of the time, I was told to wait awhile longer. For the sake of appearances, no beer was in that tub. But jars of clear liquid, discreetly covered by wrinkled brown paper bags, were retrieved occasionally from automobile trunks and truck beds and passed around.

Most everyone agrees that, at their best, North Carolina oysters are as good as any in the world. They're all basically the same species, *Crassostrea virginica*, the Eastern oyster (also known as the Atlantic or Virginia oyster), but they vary widely in size and flavor according to where in our sounds or tidal rivers they're harvested. Newport River oysters, "Masonboro clusters," "Lockwood Folly rocks," Stump Sound oysters, "Topsail selects," and Hyde County oysters all have their outspoken adherents.

North Carolina's oystering areas are located in or around our sounds in a range of saltwater and freshwater habitats. The best-tasting oysters tend to come from areas that are close to ocean inlets. That guarantees there will be saltier water at the bottom of the estuary (fresher water always layers on top) than in areas with a higher proportion of fresh water. Since oysters live on the bottom and never

Some oyster beds, like these in the estuarine Lockwood Folly River, are exposed at low tide, while others are always covered with water.
UNC-TV

move, the saltier the water at the lowest depth, the saltier the taste of the oysters. In terms of size, oysters grow faster and tend to be bigger when they're always covered by water (and are not harvested too early), whereas they tend to be smaller (though just as flavorful) if they come from shallower areas where they're exposed at low tide.

We will never again see the mountainous oyster reefs that greeted the earliest European explorers and settlers, or the thousand-year-old mounds of discarded shells left by native inhabitants. But we have come a long way back. Two major developments in recent years have begun to restore a North Carolina oyster fishery that had declined by an incredible 50 percent since the late 1800s.

The first is restoration of oyster beds and reefs through the simple expedient of putting oyster shells back into the water, rather than crushing them to surface roads and driveways or to mulch fruit trees. Oysters spawn, releasing sperm or eggs, when the water tempera-

ture reaches sixty-eight degrees. The resulting larvae, so tiny that millions will fit into the palm of a hand, float for a short while but soon sink to the bottom, looking for a hard place to attach themselves so as to grow into "spats," or baby oysters. They will never again move from that spot. The more oyster beds that are refurbished and rebuilt, the bigger the wild oyster harvests will be. Since a single oyster can filter impurities from fifty gallons of water, restoring oyster beds and increasing the oyster population is also a major part of restoring water quality in our wetlands.

The second development is the significant increase in oyster cultivation through aquaculture. Commercial oyster growers purchase larvae from hatcheries and put them into tanks containing oyster shells, so the larvae will have something hard to which they can attach themselves. Baby oysters are eventually removed from the tanks and "seeded" on to new or existing privately leased oyster beds on sound and tidal creek bottoms. The minimum size for harvesting either wild or cultivated oysters is three inches, but many growers let them mature to four inches in order to be able to furnish a more consistent-sized product to restaurants and oyster bars. At least 14 percent of North Carolina's oyster harvest now comes from bivalves cultivated through aquaculture. Stump Sound, at the north end of Topsail Island, is famous for the quality of its oysters. Nowadays, quite a few of the prized Stump Sound mollusks are commercially farmed, particularly to supply the restaurant trade.

North Carolina's wild-harvest oyster season runs roughly from October through March, which largely squares with the old proverb about eating oysters only during months containing the letter *r*. That folk saying mostly applied to the many generations during which refrigeration was lacking. But as long as they're kept at or below forty-five degrees, oysters are safe to eat year-round, assuming they haven't been harvested from beds affected by pollution or disease. As long as they're at least three inches in size, farmed oysters can be harvested any month of the year, although most are still gathered during autumn, winter, and early spring.

Since oysters spawn during the warm months, they're softer, more watery, and less flavorful during late spring and summer. If you're going to eat oysters during this period, consider having them deep-fried, rather than raw or steamed. But oyster bars and restaurants in New York and other northeastern states serve cultivated oysters, often raw, all summer long, and customers seem to love them, so go figure.

If you're in the mood for raw oysters on the half shell (which you should consume only in a commercial establishment set up to serve them that way), what should you look for? Oyster tasting, like wine tasting, is personal and subjective. It takes time to develop a discriminating palate. *Bon Appétit* offers these suggestions:

Smell the oysters first. Obviously, you'll want them to have a saltwater or ocean-evocative aroma.

Give the oysters a good visual once-over. *Bon Appétit* says, "A healthy oyster fills out the sturdy shell with fat, firm meat."

To speed the development of your oyster-tasting chops, don't drown the oysters in sauce or toppings. Try eating at least the first one "naked."

Slurp the oysters with whatever liquor is swimming on the shell (there should be some), and give them two or three chews before swallowing.

You'll need some lingo readily at hand. Be prepared to have descriptive words such as *mild*, *briny*, and *buttery* spring from your lips.

Decline to eat any half-shell oysters that look thin or watery.

Actually, North Carolinians are more likely to consume steamed or roasted oysters at an outdoor oyster roast or a down-home oyster bar than they are to eat them raw on the half shell at a fancy establishment.

Charcoal-grilled oysters on the half shell, long a Louisiana favorite, are becoming more popular in North Carolina.
UNC-TV

In April 2013, food writer Andrea Weigl published some suggestions in the *News & Observer* for throwing a successful oyster roast. Her tips are based on a personal demonstration by Matt and Ted Lee of Charleston, South Carolina, and are included in their 2006 cookbook, *The Lee Bros. Southern Cookbook*.

To serve six to eight people, you'll need a bushel of oysters, which amounts to around twelve dozen oysters, or eighteen to twenty-four per person. An old metal sign of the type I described earlier, around four feet square, will do admirably for the cooking surface, although a sheet of steel mesh will work just as well and will prove cheaper than purchasing a piece of new sheet metal and having it cut to order. Maybe someone has a steel-mesh pig cooker grate you can borrow as a surface on which to roast the oysters. Use four cinder blocks as a foundation for the grill or grate, and have a good stack of firewood on hand. You'll need more heat than typically generated by a bed of charcoal alone, so firewood is better for this purpose; you can add charcoal to the wood fire if you like. Be sure to have a metal shovel on hand for shoveling the oysters onto the grate, then transferring the cooked oysters from the grate to a table covered with newspaper. You may want a metal bucket to help with this process.

To cover the oysters for steaming, one

thoroughly soaked burlap bag or a couple of old, saturated bath towels is all you'll need. Many people skip the steaming part entirely and simply roast the oysters uncovered until the shells start to open. You'll probably have to adjust the heat and cooking time to get the texture you prefer, but roasting the oysters for about five minutes covered with burlap or six to eight minutes uncovered will put you in the ballpark.

You'll also need a pair of gloves or a couple of old kitchen towels per person to help hold the hot oysters while they're being opened. You'll need an oyster knife per person as well. A pan of melted butter (which can be kept warm on the edge of the fire grate), some bottles of your favorite hot sauce, a bottle of pepper vinegar, some crackers, paper bowls, plastic forks, and a roll of paper towels will round out your list of supplies. You'll probably have a modern cooler on hand, rather than a galvanized washtub full of hand-chipped ice, but you'll just have to live with that step down from perfection.

Ice down plenty of beer or soft drinks, according to your preference, and enjoy one of North Carolina's traditional alfresco dining experiences!

Oyster roasts are a cherished North Carolina tradition.

BOB GARNER'S SCALLOPED OYSTERS

THESE ARE A FAMILY favorite at Thanksgiving and Christmas. We sometimes forget to make them at other times during oyster season, but perhaps including this recipe will remind me!

2 tablespoons butter
1 quart oysters in liquid, divided
2 tablespoons bacon bits, divided
2½ cups finely crushed saltine crackers, divided
⅔ cup whole milk or half-and-half
1 teaspoon Worcestershire sauce
1 tablespoon dry sherry
½ cup melted butter
½ teaspoon salt
½ teaspoon pepper

Preheat oven to 350 degrees. Use the 2 tablespoons of butter to butter a shallow baking dish. Drain oysters and keep ⅓ cup of the liquid. Layer half the oysters in bottom of baking dish. Sprinkle on 1 tablespoon of the bacon bits, Cover oysters with half of the crushed crackers. Cover crackers with remaining oysters and remaining tablespoon of bacon bits. Mix together milk or half-and-half, reserved oyster liquid, Worcestershire sauce, sherry, melted butter, salt, and pepper. Pour this mixture over the layers in the dish. Cover with remaining crushed crackers and dot with additional butter if you like. Bake for about 45 minutes until nicely browned. This recipe generously serves 4.

FEATURE ATTRACTIONS

SUNNY SIDE OYSTER BAR

Widely regarded as one of the best seafood restaurants in eastern North Carolina, Williamston's Sunny Side Oyster Bar is open only during oyster season, from September through April. And regular customers warn that April can be iffy.

This restaurant, listed on the National Register of Historic Places, has been in continuous operation since 1935, although it was actually begun in 1930. The four current owners took over from the son of the founder in 1991, vowing to keep up Sunny Side's rich tradition. They have done so admirably.

In addition to steamed or raw oysters, the restaurant offers outstanding steamed shrimp, scallops, and crab legs and even has steamed broccoli available as a side dish. (As long as Sunny Side has a big ol' steamer, why not?)

When I first visited in 1970 or thereabouts, the restaurant looked a bit like a vintage country store and service station. It's been refurbished since then but is still at least partially housed in the same structure, now sided in white clapboard. There's a spacious waiting room with tables and a small bar; live music is sometimes offered in this front room on weekends. Since the restaurant doesn't take reservations, that's where patrons wait for space to open up in the back room.

There, a U-shaped oyster bar with twenty-two wooden stools is the center of action.

Sunny Side Oyster Bar
UNC-TV

There's really no kitchen. Oysters are steamed out back behind the restaurant in a boxy contraption, then carried in by the peck. Wood shavings on the floor behind the bar help keep the shuckers from losing their footing in the slippery oyster goo. No one wants anything to happen to those guys, some of whom have been around for decades and are accorded celebrity status.

Griff, Nate, or one of the other avuncular hosts will explain the system to newcomers and get them supplied with "setups": melted butter; the special, heated house cocktail sauce; saltines; and a shallow dish for the shucked oysters or other shellfish. If you're having oysters, you can order them raw or steamed to a stage varying from barely warmed to well-done. The mollusks come by the peck or half-peck; the smaller order provides fifteen to twenty-five oysters, depending on their size (they're usually pretty large).

This is no upscale raw bar, but rather a place where the owners have always been proud to say, "The ditch digger can sit down next to the millionaire, and both can have a great meal." No introduction to oysters in North Carolina is complete without a visit to Sunny Side Oyster Bar.

SUNNY SIDE OYSTER BAR

1102 Washington Street

Williamston, N.C. 27892

252-792-3416

sunnysideoysterbarnc.com

Open for dinner nightly, September
  through April

VARNAMTOWN OYSTER ROAST

Varnamtown is a tiny fishing village in Brunswick County on the banks of the Lockwood Folly River, southwest of Wilmington. There really isn't much of an identifiable village center, but the hamlet—three miles from Holden Beach—is home to Dixon Chapel United Methodist Church, which has been holding its annual fund-raising oyster roast for over sixty years. The Varnamtown Oyster Roast, as it's widely known, coincides with the opening of oyster season in late October or early November and is the only such event in the state that uses local oysters exclusively.

Varnamtown fishermen are busiest with shrimp in the summer and oysters in cooler weather. Oyster reefs in the Lockwood Folly River are covered by water at high tide and lie exposed at low tide. The oyster beds look like rocky mud flats. Licensed oystermen actually walk around on the reefs to gather the five bushels per day they're allowed to harvest; the limit is ten bushels per boat. Lockwood Folly "rocks," as they're sometimes called, are smaller oysters than some, since they aren't covered by water all the time. But locals say they have

At the Varnamtown Oyster Roast, hush puppies and sweet pickles are provided on the side. Visitors bring their own favorite sauce, oyster knife, and gloves.

great flavor and are good, salty oysters. The nearby Lockwood Folly ocean inlet separates the southern end of Oak Island from Holden Beach; it pumps plenty of salt water into the short tidal river, thereby increasing the desirable flavor of the mollusks.

The Dixon Chapel congregation is lucky to have a real oyster maven running the annual fund-raiser. Marlene Varnam, widow of Carson, now operates Carson Varnam's Shellfish Market across the road from the church building. She's been on the oyster roast committee for decades, so things always run pretty smoothly. Basically, locals and visitors from as far away as the West Coast stand in line for a half-hour and pay twenty dollars (eight dollars for children) to stand elbow to elbow with strangers and shuck their own oysters, which are roasted at high temperature (not steamed) over oak fires. Church volunteers keep the tables supplied with not only all-you-can-eat oysters but also hot hush puppies and sliced sweet pickles. Soft drinks are for sale. Patrons are expected to bring their own oyster knives, gloves, and favorite sauces. For non–oyster lovers, adult and children's fried fish plates are available, as are hot dogs and a panoply of local baked goods and crafts. The compact Lockwood Folly oysters are indeed firm, meaty, salty, and utterly delicious, and the conversation around the tables is in itself worth the price of the event.

Mushrooming development in Brunswick County and the resulting pollution led to the loss of half of the river bottom for oyster harvesting between 1972 and 2006. This trend, happily, is being turned around, thanks to a strict local water-quality plan and careful monitoring and inspection by state officials. As is happening elsewhere, a big push to replenish oyster reefs by putting empty shells back into the local waters is resulting in an oyster population that's growing once again. And that in turn contributes to better water quality because of oysters' incredible capacity for filtering impurities.

VARNAMTOWN OYSTER ROAST

Dixon Chapel United Methodist Church

190 Varnamtown Road, S.W.

Varnamtown, N.C. 28462

910-892-6025

Held around the first weekend in November; the church's Facebook page has details. https://facebook.com/pages/Dixon-Chapel-United-Methodist-Church/347823730456

HATTERAS CLAM CHOWDER

A bowl of Hatteras clam chowder
UNC-TV

OYSTER STEW, made with milk, has its place in North Carolina, but by far the most popular and widespread seafood soup or stew in the state is clam chowder. Being the cosmopolitan state that we are, we consume quite a bit of the thick, creamy New England version. Our own version of the dish is called Hatteras clam chowder.

Our variation is practically identical to the recipe served in most of Rhode Island, leading one to suspect that our Outer Banks–style clam chowder probably migrated to the area along with fishermen from farther north, or perhaps by way of shipwrecked mariners, although that wouldn't have happened in all likelihood until the late 1800s. The broth—clam juice and water, basically—is clear, and the chowder typically contains clams, bacon, potatoes, onions, and sometimes celery and carrots, along with perhaps fresh herbs and a respectable amount of pepper.

The term *chowder* probably came from the French *chaudière*, meaning cooking pot, although some insist it came from the English word *jowter*, meaning fish peddler or fishmonger. I wouldn't bet on the second possibility, considering the popularity of what would today be called chowders along certain sections of the Brittany and Normandy coasts.

Except for the substitution of clams for smoked haddock, clam chowder is remarkably similar to the Scottish soup Cullen skink, but no direct tie between the two is suspected. Foodies tend to bring up the similarity basically because they like to write or say "Cullen skink."

Clams did not become commonplace as an ingredient in chowders until the mid-1800s. Even at that time, they were reluctantly worked into recipes mainly because they were so ridiculously easy to gather. It clearly wasn't because people were wild about clams, which actually have very little taste on their own.

The native inhabitants of the northeastern part of what is now the United States ate a lot of clams, sometimes piling their clam and oyster shells into mounds more than ten feet high. But the first European settlers didn't care much for any type of fish or shellfish except eels. (Eel chowder?) During the 1620s, the Pilgrims are said to have fed clams and mussels—calling them "the meanest of God's blessings"—to their hogs. And even after clam chowder became commonplace, it was a seasonal dish, not a year-round standby. Various fish chowders that included salt pork, pilot biscuits or hardtack soaked in water or milk, onions, spices, and sometimes wine were much more common than clam chowder. (Potatoes and other vegetables such as celery and carrots seem to have been added to the ingredients much later.) Those original chowders used hard, tough sea biscuits, rather than flour, as a main ingredient and thickener. Today, that custom has been diminished to perhaps sprinkling a few oyster crackers or, farther south, crushed saltines over bowls of chowder.

By all evidence, it took the Pilgrims and other Northeasterners over two hundred years to really warm up to clam chowder. Isn't it ironic, then, that it is far more popular in the United States today than all other chowders combined? Part of the reason for its growth is that clam chowder was for many years the variety of soup most often served in restaurants on Fridays. Even though Vatican II in the 1960s did away with the requirement for Catholics to abstain from eating meat on Fridays (reducing the stricture to the Lenten season), restaurants continued serving clam chowder because of its wide acceptance.

New England clam chowder is the best-known variety. It is thicker than other types, originally because of the soaked hardtack and now because of the use of milk or cream, along with flour-and-butter thickening. This version dates to the mid-1700s, although it was another hundred years before clam chowder began to gain a toehold in the region.

Manhattan-style clam chowder, featuring a clear broth, tomato purée, and tomato pieces, is another famous variety. The name actually has nothing to do with Manhattan. The tomato-based chowder originated with Portuguese immigrants in Rhode Island, but their version caught on only in certain southern areas of the Ocean State and was pretty well despised by other Rhode Island residents. The worst insult a Rhode Islander could deliver was to call someone a New Yorker or to suggest that something came from New York. *Manhattan-style clam chowder* was thus a term of disapprobation for the variant invented by Rhode Islanders' own fellow citizens. There seem to be no recipes for Manhattan-style clam chowder before the 1930s, which means the Portuguese Rhode

Islanders probably invented it early in the twentieth century. (Since tomatoes were not commonly consumed before around 1820, they wouldn't have found their way into any sort of soup or chowder before that time.)

As a marketing gimmick, enterprising Long Island restaurateurs took advantage of the rivalry between New England–style and Manhattan-style clam chowders to develop what they named Long Island–style clam chowder, a sort of cream-of-tomato clam chowder incorporating elements of both styles. Long Island, you see, is geographically halfway between Manhattan and New England.

Other clam chowder variations include Delaware-style, which uses cubed salt pork instead of bacon, and New Jersey–style, which incorporates crab spice (Old Bay seasoning), asparagus, light cream, and sliced tomatoes, along with the more traditional ingredients. Something for everyone!

North Carolinians love to boast about their Hatteras-style clam chowder, caring little that it is likely an import from the North. The recipes below, in fact, are much more closely associated with the Outer Banks today than they are with Rhode Island. Really, we just plain stole our chowder—and got away with it, too.

For a bowl of one of the state's best versions of Hatteras clam chowder, visit Sam & Omie's, that iconic Nags Head breakfast place founded in 1937 by a couple of fishermen; call 252-441-7366 or visit www.samandomies.net.

HATTERAS CLAM CHOWDER WITH FRESH CLAMS

3 dozen clams
8 ounces thick-cut bacon (or salt pork)
1 large onion, peeled and diced
8 large potatoes, peeled and cubed
3 quarts water
salt and pepper to taste

Rinse clam shells under running water. Open clams over a bowl to catch the juice. Using a slotted spoon, separate clams from juice. Reserve juice. Put clams in the freezer until they're just barely frozen. Chop clams by hand or with a food processor.

In a large pot, fry bacon until it's nicely browned and all the fat is rendered. Remove bacon and set aside, leaving the drippings. Add onions and cook over low heat for 5 minutes until they're translucent but not brown. Add bacon back to pot, along with clams, reserved clam juice, potatoes, and water. Season with salt and pepper, but take it easy here, as clams are already salty. Bring pot to a boil and simmer for 1½ hours; the longer the chowder cooks, the more flavorful it will be. To thicken chowder, mash some of the potatoes against the side of the pot as the chowder simmers. If you like, garnish each bowl of chowder with chopped fresh parsley.

This recipe serves 6 to 8. It comes courtesy of www.obxconnection.com.

HATTERAS CLAM CHOWDER WITH CANNED CLAMS

8 slices bacon

1 large onion, chopped

5 stalks celery, sliced

4 carrots, sliced

1 tablespoon vegetable oil (or bacon drippings)

4 cups white potatoes, peeled and cubed

3 16-ounce cans of clams

2 quarts clam juice

1 teaspoon dried thyme

½ teaspoon ground pepper

In a frying pan, cook bacon crisp; remove from pan and crumble. In a large pot over medium heat, cook onions, celery, and carrots in oil or bacon drippings until they begin to soften. Stir in potatoes, clams, clam juice, thyme, pepper, and bacon. Bring to a boil, reduce heat, and simmer for 20 minutes until potatoes are tender.

This recipe serves 8. It comes from ODella Romaine, courtesy of AllRecipes.com.

Scuppernongs
AND
MUSCADINES
AMERICA'S FIRST
CULTIVATED GRAPES

The first cultivated grapes in America came from North Carolina, so it's no surprise that the scuppernong—a bronze-colored variety of the muscadine grape—is our state fruit.

Giovanni da Verrazano, the Italian navigator who explored the Cape Fear River Valley in 1524, wrote in his logbook that he saw "many vines growing naturally there." (When Leif Ericson discovered America five centuries earlier and called it Vinland or Vineland, it could have been because of the plentiful vines of native muscadine grapes he observed.)

Captains Philip Amadas and Arthur Barlowe, exploring on behalf of Sir Walter Raleigh, wrote in 1584 that the coast of North Carolina was "so full of grapes as the very beating and surge of the sea overflowed them. . . . In all the world like abundance is not to be found." Even though Amadas and Barlowe may have been referring to Sargassum seaweed (which has berry-like clusters), Governor Ralph Lane shortly afterward described North Carolina to Sir Walter Raleigh by saying, "We have discovered the main to be the goodliest soil under the cope of heaven, abounding with sweet trees that bring rich and pleasant grapes of such greatness, yet wild, as France, Spain nor Italy hath no greater."

Early explorers and settlers were familiar with the French muscat grape, used in making muscatel wine. (The word *muscat* derives from the Latin *muscus*, describing the smell of a male musk deer.) So the settlers called the musk-scented, sweet native grapes they found here by the name of the European sweet grapes they had previously known, and *muscat* eventually became *muscadine* in common parlance. Native Americans consumed both the fruit and the juice—and also dried and preserved the grapes—long before Europeans arrived on the scene.

Although purple and black varieties are usually called muscadines, most North Carolinians refer to any bronze- or greenish-hued muscadines as scuppernongs. That's because

Most North Carolinians refer to any bronze- or greenish-hued muscadines as scuppernongs.
DUPLIN TOURISM

many cuttings of what was first simply called "the big white grape" were planted and cultivated during the 1700s around the Ascupernung, a short river in Tyrell and Washington counties that flows into Albemarle Sound. By 1800, the spelling of the river's name, as well as that of a small town nearby, became Scuppernong. Soon, the name of the town and river was universally applied to the grape variety that became widely grown in the area.

Muscadines, including scuppernongs, have four large seeds and tough skins and are described in the vernacular as being "about the size of a hog's eye"—maybe an inch and a half in diameter. The grapes grow in loose clusters, rather than conventional bunches, so they are traditionally harvested as individual berries by being shaken from the vines. The grapes' abundant juice—musky and fruity—makes great-tasting wine, jam, and jelly, and the hulls, when separated from the juice, pulp, and seeds, make a prized pie filling once they're tenderized by slow cooking.

Muscadines are not only one of the sweet-

est grape varieties in the world but also one of the healthiest. The hot, humid climates where they thrive, like that of eastern North Carolina, produce fungal diseases. Muscadines respond to this stress by producing extra antioxidants to protect themselves. As a result, studies have shown that muscadine wine contains seven times more disease-fighting antioxidant properties than European varieties.

In 1995, the television show *60 Minutes* aired a segment on the health benefits of drinking muscadine wine. Duplin Winery, which had experienced an up-and-down existence for more than twenty years at that time, saw a dramatic increase in sales following the report. The winery has continued to grow steadily ever since, becoming not only North Carolina's largest winery but the twenty-fourth-largest in the country. Other wineries concentrating on muscadines have also taken root in Duplin County.

Experts say the muscadine or scuppernong should be eaten as follows. Place the grape in your mouth with the stem scar facing upward. When you bite down, the pulp and juice will burst through the thick skin into your mouth, after which the skin and seeds can be discarded—or swallowed for maximum health benefit, since antioxidants are found in the skin, pulp, juice, and seeds!

The official state toast refers to the Old North State as a place "where the scuppernong perfumes the breeze at night." There may be no other fruit with such strong personal associations for so many North Carolina natives.

Duplin County is home to the annual North Carolina Muscadine Harvest Festival, which includes a cooking contest. Cooks may enter dishes using at least one cup of muscadine grapes, juice, or wine in five categories: Salads and Appetizers; Breads and Muffins; Entrées; Desserts; and Jams, Jellies, and Preserves. The dishes are judged on creative use of muscadines, flavor, texture, ease of preparation, and general appearance. Here are some of the winning recipes from recent years.

SPARKLING OATMEAL MUFFINS

THIS RECIPE in the Breads and Muffins category—for not-too-sweet, moist, flavorful muffins perfect for a fall morning—is from Annie Clawson of Ivanhoe.

1½ to 2 cups scuppernong or muscadine red grapes
1½ cups water
1 tablespoon honey
1½ cups all-purpose flour, sifted
½ cup quick-cook oatmeal
2 teaspoons wheat germ
2 teaspoons baking powder
½ teaspoon baking soda
½ teaspoon cinnamon
½ teaspoon salt
1 egg
1 cup sparkling muscadine wine
¼ cup buttermilk
¼ cup brown sugar, packed
3 tablespoons butter, melted

Preheat oven to 400 degrees. Grease a 12-cup muffin pan. Remove hulls from grapes and measure out 1 cup of hulls. Squeeze the pulp of the grapes to extract the juice. Boil hulls in water, honey, and juice from the grapes for about 30 minutes until tender. Drain, then chop hulls into small pieces.

Sift flour into a large mixing bowl. Add oatmeal, wheat germ, baking powder, baking soda, cinnamon, and salt and whisk together thoroughly. Lightly whisk egg in a medium bowl. Add wine, buttermilk, brown sugar, butter, and chopped grape hulls and mix until thoroughly combined. Add liquid mixture to flour mixture. Mix with a wooden spoon until ingredients are just moistened. Do not overmix. Place approximately ¼ cup batter into each muffin cup. Bake for about 15 minutes until lightly browned on top. Let cool for 3 to 5 minutes, then remove from muffin pan.

CHICKEN VEGETABLE KABOBS WITH MUSCADINE BARBECUE SAUCE

THIS RECIPE in the Entrées category is from Nancy Wilson of Kenansville.

KABOBS

4 12-inch wooden skewers
1 tablespoon coarsely chopped fresh
  rosemary
2 tablespoons olive oil
1 cup muscadine pepper jelly
½ teaspoon salt
½ teaspoon loosely packed orange
  zest
½ teaspoon pepper
6 boneless, skinless chicken thighs
  (a little over 1 pound), cut into 1½-
  inch pieces
1 small zucchini, cut into 1½-inch
  pieces
1 small summer squash, cut into 1½-
  inch pieces
1 red bell pepper, trimmed and cut
  into 1½-inch pieces
1 yellow bell pepper, trimmed and cut
  into 1½-inch pieces
1 green bell pepper, trimmed and cut
  into 1½-inch pieces

MUSCADINE BARBECUE SAUCE

¾ cup mayonnaise
2 tablespoons white vinegar
1 tablespoon Duplin Winery Hatteras
  Red Wine

1½ teaspoons pepper
1½ teaspoons spicy brown mustard
½ teaspoon sugar
½ teaspoon salt

Soak wooden skewers for 30 minutes. Preheat grill to 350 to 400 degrees (medium-high). Whisk rosemary and next 5 ingredients together in a bowl. Add chicken and remaining kabob ingredients and stir together to coat. Thread chicken and vegetables alternately on skewers and discard marinade. Grill kabobs, covered, for 12 to 14 minutes until done, turning occasionally. Let stand 5 minutes.

Stir together all sauce ingredients; the recipe yields about 1 cup and can be refrigerated for up to 1 week. Serve sauce with kabobs.

MUSCADINE NACHOS

THIS ENTRY in the Salads and Appetizers category is from Fran Andre of Beulaville.

1 pound lean ground beef
1 small package taco seasoning
1 cup muscadine red wine
3 tablespoons heavy cream
medium-sized bag tortilla chips
⅓ cup diced tomatoes
⅓ cup salsa, divided
2 cups shredded lettuce
¼ cup shredded cheddar cheese
¼ cup black beans
¼ cup sour cream

Brown and drain ground beef, then add taco seasoning, wine, and heavy cream. Let simmer 5 minutes. Remove from stove and layer with chips, tomatoes, salsa, and lettuce. Then make another layer and top with cheese, black beans, sour cream, and salsa.

MUSCADINE GRAPE HULL PIE

THIS RECIPE in the Desserts category is from Tilda Beasley of Warsaw.

¾ cup sugar
¾ cup flour
5 eggs, separated
1 quart muscadine grape hulls
2 tablespoons butter

2 teaspoons vanilla, divided
2 9-inch pie shells, cooked
½ cup plus 2 tablespoons sugar

Mix together ¾ cup sugar, flour, and egg yolks in a saucepan, then add grape hulls. Cook mixture until thickened. Stir butter and 1 teaspoon of vanilla into thickened filling. Pour filling into pie shells.

Beat reserved egg whites until firm, then mix in ½ cup plus 2 tablespoons sugar and remaining teaspoon of vanilla. Divide meringue to cover tops of pies. Place pies in a preheated 350-degree oven for about 10 minutes until golden brown on top.

Muscadine Grape Hull Pie, baked with either a meringue topping or a traditional crust, is a Duplin County favorite.
AMY C. EVANS

FEATURE ATTRACTIONS

COUNTRY SQUIRE

The Country Squire is probably the most unique restaurant and inn in eastern North Carolina. It's located on a rural stretch of N.C. 50 between Warsaw and Kenansville. But once you're on the grounds of "the Squire," as it's known to the staff and local residents, you'll be more or less in a world of your own.

The place rambles. The restaurant opened in a log-cabin-like structure in 1961, which even then was part of a complex of buildings and portions of buildings dating to the early 1800s. Some recycled building materials even remained from the eighteenth century. The log structure has since been completely enclosed by other additions, and the whole kit and caboodle is surrounded by a dense stand of trees and attractive grounds that include brick walkways, a fountain, creeping ivy, decorative benches, and a gazebo. The separate, adjacent inn has a half-timbered English/Scottish look to it and, as some guests have noted, "could use a little updating." But it's clean, comfortable, and well maintained. Personally, I wouldn't change a thing.

The Country Squire also has a definite Scottish sound to it, thanks to owner Iris Lennon's brogue. Lennon emigrated from Scotland many years ago and worked in various capacities at the Squire for decades before assuming ownership.

Although the place has several dining rooms, each with different ambiance and décor, the waitresses all wear long dresses and aprons. The food is generally top-notch; prime rib, steaks, beef tips, marinated Korean beef, marinated turkey, and Caesar salad (prepared tableside) are some of the dinner menu standouts.

Although the Country Squire complex has a winery on the grounds, its wines were, until 2012, produced mostly from imported grapes, rather than local muscadines. It has now established its own muscadine vineyard and—supplemented by some off-site acreage—provides grapes for muscadine wine production in addition to the other vintages. The vineyard at the Squire also serves as a bucolic site for outdoor weddings. The Tartan Gift Shop carries local muscadine jams and jellies and Country Squire–branded marinades and dressings, in addition to art, jewelry, and decorative accessories. A wine-tasting room extends off the gift shop.

The Squire's mascot, Willy, is a full-body (but only half-sized) suit of armor that greets visitors stepping into the charming, compact anteroom/lobby. Those arriving for dinner will find a complimentary relish tray and, on fall and winter evenings, a welcoming fire in the fireplace. The place supposedly has a resident ghost. Although guests more than likely will not see it, they'll definitely hear about it before they're done.

Country Squire Restaurant, Winery, and Vintage Inn
MIKE ONIFFREY

COUNTRY SQUIRE RESTAURANT, WINERY, AND VINTAGE INN

748 N.C. 24/N.C. 50

Warsaw, N.C. 28398

910-296-1727

www.countrysquireinn.com

DUPLIN WINERY

Make no mistake about it, Rose Hill's Duplin Winery is not trying to imitate or duplicate anything in California. Jonathan Fussell, one of two brothers in his family's second generation of winery operators, says, "We sell sweet wines. That's what we're good at." His brother, Dave, adds that Duplin Winery concentrates on producing sweet, fruity wines that taste like grapes eaten right off the vine. Since muscadines are one of the earth's sweetest varieties, Duplin's wines don't have to be aged, unlike others made from grapes that start out tasting relatively bitter.

Most people think muscadine wines, red and white alike, taste better chilled because the cold brings out the fruitiness—something the winery is trying to emphasize, not hide. Wine snobbery aside, the "cool, sweet, and easy" Duplin vintages simply taste good and are refreshing to a great many residents of North Carolina and other states that regularly test their populations with hot, humid conditions. Ironically, it's that same steamy climate that toughens the grapes' skins, protecting the sweet interiors, and also compels the muscadines to develop healthful properties.

Duplin Winery had been in existence for twenty-three years, many of them tough, before the pivotal, aforementioned *60 Minutes* report turned things around. One of the winery's founders, Dave Fussell Sr., lost pretty much everything, including his home, after the North Carolina General Assembly first created a tax break for North Carolina wine producers and then saw it overturned by the United States Supreme Court as unconstitutional. Duplin Winery had been started largely because of the tax break. When profits plummeted after that benefit disappeared, years of uncertainty and financial loss followed.

All that has turned around for the winery, which sells more wine than any other in the Southeast. The place still is no showplace, although it has made improvements to the landscaping. The building housing The Bistro,

The tasting room at Duplin Winery

the tasting room, and the gift shop still looks like a warehouse—which is exactly what it was before it became Duplin's original winery.

Out on Interstate 40, some eighteen billboards—adorned with cutouts representing bottles of Duplin Wine and its familiar Hatteras Lighthouse logo—will direct you to Exit 380 and Duplin Winery. You'll pass acres of vineyards and "the World's Largest Frying Pan" on Rose Hill's Sycamore Street before getting there. Once you arrive, expect to be greeted with courteous hospitality and an opportunity to taste at least one sweet beverage you'll know is actually good for you. Jonathan Fussell, who runs Duplin's Bistro, tasting room, and gift shop, may be personally on hand to intone, "If you close your eyes and sniff, a glass of muscadine wine smells like a glassful of grapes."

DUPLIN WINERY

505 North Sycamore Street
Rose Hill, N.C. 28458
800-774-9634
duplinwinery.com
Open Monday through Saturday

NORTH CAROLINA MUSCADINE HARVEST FESTIVAL

This annual festival takes place in mid- to late September; tickets can be ordered online at the event's website.

Held at the Duplin County Events Cen-

ter at the fairgrounds in Kenansville, the North Carolina Muscadine Harvest Festival is a Friday and Saturday event focused on popular beach-type bands and other musical groups; food, wine, and merchandise vendors; a cooking contest; and an amateur winemaking contest. Both the cooking and winemaking contests involve products made at home and brought in for judging on Friday; the winners are announced on Saturday.

Tailgating spots not far from the performance area are rented on a first-come, first-served basis. Patrons are allowed to bring in their own food, beer, and liquor "as long as it is concealed." Tellingly, attendees are not permitted to bring in their own wine!

But why would they? It's still hot in Duplin County in September, so some of the "cool, sweet, and easy" muscadine wine sold by festival vendors is just the ticket.

NORTH CAROLINA MUSCADINE HARVEST FESTIVAL

P.O. Box 175
Kenansville, N.C. 28349
910-290-0525
www.muscadineharvestfestival.com

Ocracoke Fig Cake was reportedly invented during the 1950s by substituting fig preserves in a date cake recipe.

OCRACOKE FIG CAKE

THE ANCIENTS COMPOSED poetry and song about figs. Buddha is said to have obtained enlightenment while sitting under a fig tree.

Figs are also one of the first plants mentioned in the Bible. According to the biblical account, Jesus searched for or was given only two specific foods when he was hungry: figs and fish. Ocracoke Island on the Outer Banks is famous for both. So if Jesus wanted some mmm-mmm in North Carolina, where might he have gone? I'm just sayin' . . .

Ocracoke has a mere seven hundred or so year-round residents, but that number swells to thousands during the tourist season, even though the relatively undeveloped island is accessible only by ferry. Visitors come for the miles of pristine beaches, the unhurried pace of life, the fishing—and also because the island produces special deliciousness in the form of fig preserves and its widely celebrated Ocracoke fig cake, a moist, dark spice cake that's sometimes served with cream cheese icing or, during the holidays, with hard sauce, like plum pudding.

Most old Ocracoke houses have fig trees brought by the early settlers. Figs have been cultivated on the island since the 1700s. Natives like to say the old trees stop bearing within three years of the time someone moves out. Loneliness? Local fig expert and florist Chester Lynn says it isn't that, but rather that there's no one to regularly fertilize the trees with food scraps and cooking liquids, or to mulch around the base of the trees with oyster and clam shells.

There's no question that Ocracokers have a special knack for growing, preserving, and baking with figs—so much so that the island has an annual fig festival. At least a dozen varieties of figs are grown on the island, some with familiar names and some with no names. The well-known Brown Turkey and Celeste types are the most common; locals also use names like *Sugar* and *Blue* to refer to specific offshoots of Celeste figs. There's also a variety named for nearby Portsmouth Island and one that's called Pound, since, according to Chester Lynn, "it can weigh nearly a pound."

If you're looking for pure gustatory pleasure, you'll want to sample some Ocracoke fig cake. Chester Lynn says that before the 1950s, when the late Margaret Garrish invented the current iteration of the dessert, an Ocracoke fig cake probably consisted of a basic yellow cake with lemon-infused fig preserves spread between the layers. Lynn maintains that Garrish unalterably changed the paradigm when she simply substituted fig preserves for dates in a recipe for date cake.

The island has held an annual Fourth of July fig cake bake-off during recent years. The contests have tended to be won by bakers for whom fig cake is no mere occasional experiment. One winner in the Traditional category is Della Gaskill, who is a stone fig expert. She not only sells fig plants at her nursery but also ships fig preserves, crafts, and other treasures all over the world from her shop, Woccocon Nursery and Gifts. Or how about Annie Louise Gaskins, another Traditional category winner, who, as the owner of the Thurston House Inn, bakes a fig cake at least every other day? Who would want to go up against Annie in a bake-off? Gaynelle Tillett of Ocracoke Seafood Company is another well-known Ocracoke fig cake baker. While she hasn't, as far as I know, won the bake-off, she does sell and ship her version all over the country.

She'll also be ready to supply Jesus with both figs and fish, should he show up to inquire.

OCRACOKE FIG CAKE

CAKE

3 eggs
1½ cups sugar
1 cup salad oil
1 teaspoon baking soda, dissolved in a little hot water
2 cups flour
1 teaspoon nutmeg
1 teaspoon allspice
1 teaspoon cinnamon
1 teaspoon salt
½ cup buttermilk
1 teaspoon vanilla
1 cup chopped whole-fig preserves
1 cup chopped nuts

FROSTING

8-ounce package cream cheese, room temperature
½ cup unsalted butter, room temperature
1 teaspoon vanilla
1 pound confectioners' sugar

Beat eggs; add sugar, oil, and baking soda. After sifting dry ingredients, add to egg mixture alternately with buttermilk. Add vanilla and fold in figs and nuts. Pour into a greased oblong pan and bake at 325 degrees for 45 minutes to 1 hour, or pour into a well-greased tube pan and bake at 350 degrees just a little longer.

Combine frosting ingredients in a medium bowl and beat until light and fluffy. Frost cake and serve.

This recipe comes courtesy of the *Ocracoke Island Journal*.

Barbecue
AN EVOLVING ORTHODOXY

North Carolinians have been enjoying pit-cooked pork barbecue since the earliest settlers arrived to find Native Americans already practicing the smoky art. But while the affinity for one of our favorite foods is as strong as it has ever been, the state's barbecue landscape has seen significant changes in recent years. Regional paradigms in cuts of meat and sauces still exist, but they're shifting. Changes in pit design and the incorporation of cooking methods from the Midwest and West have begun to change the flavor of our barbecue. Beef brisket, ribs, chicken, and turkey are finding their way on to more and more barbecue menus. Responding to the explosive growth of local brewing, quite a few barbecue restaurants now serve alcohol. Newer barbecue eateries are often more upscale than older ones. And chain barbecue restaurants are springing up.

Let me begin, though, with the original ways that established North Carolina's rich—and dual—barbecue heritage.

Whole pigs have been cooked over live coals for nearly three and a half centuries in eastern North Carolina. Hernando De Soto and other Spanish explorers brought pigs to what would become the southeastern United States during the 1500s. The hogs were adaptable to the hot, humid climate and were able to forage in the woods, surviving and even thriving on acorns and wild roots. Over time, the pigs began to go back to nature, essentially becoming part of the wild game available to Native Americans.

The Indian peoples of the Caribbean islands and North America commonly built frameworks of green sticks over beds of coals on which to smoke and barbecue all types of meat and fish. This is the actual origin of our word *barbecue*. The Spanish approximation of the indigenous word for those early wooden grills was *barbacoa*. A similar expression used by North American tribes also found its way into English as *barbacu*. Since then have come all the various spellings and abbreviations: barbecue, barbeque, Bar-B-Que, Bar-B-Q, Bar-B-Cue, and BBQ.

In the early seventeenth century, English and Scots-Irish settlers in Virginia and northeastern North Carolina found Native Americans slowly roasting whole hogs and quickly adopted the cooking method for themselves. The old traditions and practices were then stubbornly, if sporadically, maintained for over three centuries. As late as the 1950s, some eastern North Carolinians were still digging pits and shoveling live coals into them in order to cook whole pigs, which were laid across green saplings supported by the edges of the pits, thus serving as grills. Today, in the most rustic circumstances, it is more common to use cinder blocks to build an eighteen-inch-high pit from the ground up and to use some sort of metal grill, rather than green sticks, to support the cooking hog. But the entire pig-cooking process hasn't changed dramatically over the centuries.

Pork shoulders, rather than entire pigs, have been cooked in similar pit arrangements for at least a couple of hundred years in the Piedmont and western foothills of North Carolina, although not so much in the mountains. (For whatever reason, the North Carolina mountains have never had much of a barbecue tradition until recently; it now exists primarily in restaurants serving the tourist trade and at one notable barbecue gathering, the Blue Ridge Barbecue Festival in Polk County, west of Shelby.) The preference for pork shoulders was rooted in the heavy influx of German settlers into the Piedmont. As they poured into the state during the mid-eighteenth century via the Great Wagon Road from Pennsylvania, they brought with them a strong liking for the taste of pork shoulders, the darkest and fattiest meat on the pig. The pork shoulders they consumed were cooked over coals, of course, but at that time they

were more likely to be braised in a pot with some sort of apple-flavored sauce, rather than "barbacu'd" Indian-style.

It wasn't until the early 1900s that barbecued pork shoulders, pit-cooked over hardwood coals, really came into their own as a specialty of the central North Carolina Piedmont, particularly around Lexington and Salisbury. A small group of veteran barbecue cooks became locally known for cooking pork shoulders on backyard barbecue pits and selling the meat to customers who carried it home to eat. Before long, some of those barbecuers started setting up temporary canvas-topped stands on the courthouse square in Lexington and in other locations. During the week-long sessions of circuit court and at other public observances and celebrations, what later became known as "Lexington-style" barbecue evolved into a popular tradition. Almost to a man, the early barbecue entrepreneurs were the descendants of the original German settlers, propagating the German fondness for pork shoulders in their own way.

The original sauce developed in the American colonies was a vinegar-pepper concoction popular throughout the thirteen colonies. It basically contained, as it still does, vinegar, water, black pepper, red pepper, and a fairly significant amount of salt. Tomatoes were not consumed during colonial days to anywhere near the degree they are today; the first published recipe for tomato ketchup didn't show up until 1820. So it isn't surprising that the first barbecue sauce didn't contain tomato purée, as so many do today. African slaves are thought to have developed the vinegar-

The author picking a whole pig
FRANK GREEN

pepper sauce, which was used as both a mopping sauce during cooking and a condiment for dipping barbecued meats. The vinegar penetrates the meat fibers and helps keep the texture of the fat from becoming overwhelming on the palate. These days, this basic vinegary dressing is still the favorite throughout North Carolina's coastal plain. Chopped and pulled-pork barbecue there has a pronounced tang from the vinegar and a piquant spiciness from the pepper mixture. For folks who grew up with other regional styles of barbecue, it's often an acquired taste.

During much of the eighteenth and nineteenth centuries, vinegar-pepper barbecue sauce was also popular in the North Carolina Piedmont and anywhere else barbecue was cooked. But in the early 1900s, some Piedmont barbecuers began to subtly alter the sauce by adding tomato ketchup and a little sugar. Commercially produced ketchup became widely available not long after the turn of the century. Adding modest amounts of it to the vinegar-pepper sauce created a variation that today is known as "Lexington dip" or "Piedmont dip." It's quite common—but also quite inaccurate—to hear that Lexington- or Piedmont-style barbecue and its sauce are "tomato-based." The ketchup does add sweetness and flavorings such as allspice, and it obviously changes the color of the sauce, but the dip—really a light tomato sauce—is still a fairly thin, tart dressing based more on vinegar than tomato, although it does tend to become thicker as one moves farther west in North Carolina and across Tennessee to the Mississippi River and beyond. Lexington dip

came into being to create a sweet-and-sour effect that fit the German taste for apple-flavored sauce as a dressing for pork shoulders. It isn't generally found anywhere outside the North Carolina Piedmont.

For nearly a century, the only major development in North Carolina barbecue practice involved a gradual increase in the use of gas or electric "pits" at some restaurants. These cooking devices are basically ovens in which meat can be cooked at a constant low-and-slow temperature. While they cut a lot of the mess, work, and expense involved in cooking over coals from live fires, they also eliminated much of the flavor derived from those coals and the attending smoke. They became more commonplace in eastern North Carolina barbecue joints than those in the Piedmont. That's probably because eastern pit masters figured they could more easily mask any loss in pit-cooked flavor with the livelier seasonings contained in their piquant sauce. Many entrants in eastern barbecue competitions began using gas to fire their portable pits because the ease of setting and holding a constant, low temperature allowed them to produce a more perfectly browned pig, a major criterion in eastern competitive barbecue judging.

This type of gas or electric pit is now mostly on the way out, at least in many restaurants, and other changes are in the wind. One way to explain the coming shifts is to describe some historic barbecue restaurants that have changed very little.

Today, long-established eastern-style barbecue joints that pit-cook whole hogs over live coals—wood, charcoal, or a combination

Lexington Barbecue pit-cooks whole pork shouldlers over oak and hickory wood.

of the two—are few in number. The Sky-light Inn and Bum's in Ayden; Wilbur's and Grady's in the Goldsboro area; Stephenson's in Willow Spring, near Benson; and B's in Greenville all continue to cook over live coals. A few one-day-a-week places still do as well. Wilbur's mixes in quite a few pork shoulders in addition to whole hogs, while Stephenson's cooks no whole hogs at all, although its shoul-

ders are seasoned in a no-nonsense eastern style. Nearly all other barbecue restaurants in eastern North Carolina either use straight-forward gas or electric pits, cook on a wood smoker, or employ some sort of combination cookery. Most of them cook pork shoulders rather than whole hogs so they experience better yield and exercise tighter control over the amount of meat cooked at any one time.

Parker's in Wilson, for example, uses live charcoal beneath the meat and gas burners over the meat at the same time.

The older, wood-burning barbecue joints in the Piedmont (practically no charcoal is burned there) are too numerous to name, although a few iconic restaurants come immediately to mind: Lexington Barbecue in Lexington, Stamey's in Greensboro, Allen and Son in Chapel Hill, and Red Bridges Barbecue Lodge in Shelby. Chip Stamey still oversees the live-coal cooking of pork shoulders in an impressively expansive pit house outside his landmark restaurant in Greensboro, across from the Greensboro Coliseum. His grandfather, Piedmont barbecue pioneer Warner Stamey, opened his first barbecue restaurant in Lexington in 1930. Chip probably speaks for all the iconic, tradition-preserving Piedmont restaurants, as well as the owners of numerous lesser-known wood-burners, in saying, "I think it's very important to keep the past alive. I think the old ways are the best ways. We've experimented at times with the ways other people were doing it, just to see what it was like, and I think the product is just not the same. So we're going to keep doing it the old way for as long as we can."

Nearly all the restaurants cooking either eastern-style whole-hog barbecue or Lexington-sauced pork shoulders over live coals have been around for many years. But a few newer places are also devoted to pit-cooking barbecue the old-fashioned way. Hillsborough BBQ Company, for example, went to considerable trouble to build wood-burning pits for its restaurant. As is the practice at Lexington Barbecue, whose pits served as the models for the ones at the Hillsborough restaurant, logs are burned down to coals in a fireplace. The embers are regularly spread by shovel beneath the slow-roasting Boston butts cut from the pork shoulders. The Pit Authentic Barbecue, with locations in Raleigh and Durham, is another newer enterprise that is committed to the old school of barbecue cooking. Owner Greg Hatem declares, "The tradition here is the same as it's been for 350 years. It's the same way we learned to do it growing up in Halifax County. In Raleigh, we're cooking whole hogs over live coals, and that's the way it should be done in the coastal plain. In Durham, though, you're in the beginning of the Piedmont, so we also wanted to offer the Lexington touch there." The Pit's two locations may be the fanciest barbecue restaurants in the entire country, boasting bars, valet parking, and upscale lighting and décor.

For decades, North Carolina restaurants either cooked their barbecue over live coals or used electric or gas cookers. Now, though, wood smokers are common at many barbecue restaurants, among them Charlie's Barbecue and Grille in Clayton. At Charlie's, an electric element heats a handful of bagged wood chips to produce a cloud of smoke that swirls around several shelves of Boston butts roasting in a stainless-steel smoker resembling a small refrigerator. Charlie Carden, who retired from the North Carolina Highway Patrol after thirty years to run the restaurant with his wife, Kim, says, tongue in cheek, "We don't like to kill as many trees as some folks do. We like to cook our barbecue low and slow, at around 250 degrees, and then we let the meat rest after cooking for a couple of hours. By that time, it's just falling off the bone."

As some of the older hands point out, though, there is a major difference between wood smoking and pit cooking. Chip Stamey describes his restaurant's old-school process this way: "Pit cooking is where we take the hardwood coals that have burned down from the fire in the fireplace and lay them up directly under the meat. First, you get the smoke coming up around the meat. Second, you get the juices dripping on the coals, which adds another whole layer of flavor. When that aroma goes drifting across the parking lot from our pit house, customers start coming in the door."

When barbecue is done on a wood smoker, a cooking implement that came to widespread popularity in Texas, no coals are directly under the meat, and no juice drips down to produce little puffs of heavenly scented barbecue steam. Sometimes, a log fire is started from scratch. Other times, an eighteen-inch section of pipe full of wood is heated from the outside by an intensely hot gas flame. Or a cup or two of wood chips is heated by an electric coil. But regardless of the size or location of the fire and smoke, it is always offset from the meat. Many smokers are designed so that shelves of meat rotate through a smoke chamber much like the gondolas of a Ferris wheel.

Smokers are designed to bathe barbecued meats in smoke, but they are distinct from the directly-over-the-coals pit cooking that helped build North Carolina's barbecue reputation. One way to describe the difference is to point out that smokers provide a more pronounced smoke taste (and more of the attendant red or pink color) than does pit cooking, but that they don't offer any of the grilled taste produced by hissing, spitting juices falling onto hot coals.

Nearly all of the several barbecue chains in North Carolina serve a smoked style of barbecue not native to the Tar Heel State. But one chain, Smithfield's Chicken 'N Bar-B-Q, began with the flavor profile of eastern-style, vinegar-sauced barbecue and built a wide array of locations, situating them all in the very region of the state where the company's signature dish originated. It's a rare concept: creating a regional chain that serves regionally authentic, culturally appropriate food.

As technology advances and the pace of life increases, there seems to be a widespread desire to hold on to North Carolina's rich barbecue heritage, although some of its defining characteristics are becoming blurred. Even with the changes in cooking methods, décor, ambiance, and menu variety at many of the state's barbecue restaurants, we North Carolinians still clearly love our 'cue.

CHARCOAL-COOKED PULLED PORK

You can cook pretty authentic Lexington-style pulled pork at home on a simple Weber kettle grill or any covered barbecue grill. It's an all-day process, but one that isn't labor intensive, so it's perfect for a day when you're

Whole hog or pork shoulder, big hunks of North Carolina barbecue always invite "picking."
UNC-TV

puttering around the house. To serve at 6 P.M., you'll need to start at 9 A.M. to be on the safe side.

You'll notice I don't use any temperature guidelines in my instructions. Sorry—I always go by appearance and feel. This is a recipe where it's hard to go wrong if you follow your own judgment. You'll feel like a genuine pit master when—not if—you pull it off successfully!

You'll need the following equipment: a 22-inch Weber kettle or similar covered charcoal grill; a second grill or container in which to light coals; 10 pounds of high-quality hardwood charcoal (I prefer Kingsford); a bag of hickory wood chunks (not chips); a charcoal lighting chimney; newspaper; a small shovel or scoop; barbecue tongs for handling char-

coal briquettes; heavy-duty rubber gloves; and a cutting board.

table salt
6- to 7-pound Boston butt roast
Bob Garner's Lexington-Style Dip
 (see page 72)

Generously salt the exposed meat portion of the Boston butt and leave it out at room temperature for a half-hour or so while you prepare the charcoal fire. Clean any old ash or coals from the bottom of the grill and make sure any ventilation slots at or near the bottom of the grill are open. Light 5 pounds of charcoal using a charcoal chimney and newspaper. Wait until the briquettes are entirely covered with gray ash. Arrange the charcoal in

2 even piles pushed up against opposite sides of the grill. Arrange 10 to 12 briquettes evenly in the center. Gently place 2 hickory chunks on top of each pile of charcoal. (You can soak these in water ahead of time if you like, but it isn't really necessary, since they seldom flame up as long as the cover is on the grill.) When the briquettes begin to smoke, put the cooking grate in place and set the shoulder—meat side down, skin side up—on the grate directly over the coals in the center. Place the kettle cover on the grill, leaving the ventilation holes totally open. As soon as the meat is on the fire and covered, light another dozen briquettes in the charcoal chimney so they'll be ready to add to the charcoal piles in the grill in around 30 minutes.

When the second batch of coals is completely covered in gray ash, carefully transfer them to the grill, adding 6 briquettes to each side. (Some grills, including the Weber, have openings on either side of the grate so you can add coals without removing the grate. You should be able to easily drop them onto the side piles.) Lay 2 more hickory chunks atop the fresh coals on each side, replacing the lid as quickly as possible to prevent a flare-up. (A small army-type shovel or entrenching tool is ideal for transferring coals, although any similar scoop will suffice. You can use tongs, but it will take longer to transfer coals 1 at a time.) Continue adding 6 fully lit briquettes and 2 hickory chunks on each side of the grill every half-hour or so. You won't need to add more coals to the center, directly under the meat, since the pork will become nicely browned without them. Do not lift the lid to peek in between the additions of coals, as this will cause significant heat loss and slow the cooking time. Remember, "If you're lookin', you ain't cookin.'"

Around 4 P.M., or after the Boston butt has been on the grill for around 6 hours, turn it so the meat side is facing up. This is when you'll need heavy-duty rubber gloves. It's important to keep adding coals and wood chunks on a regular basis so the temperature doesn't drop too low. But depending on your feeling about how the cooking process is proceeding, based on the color and "give" of the meat, you can reduce the number of briquettes added to each side to 4 or 5.

After another hour and a half of cooking, both the exposed meat and the skin should have turned a deep reddish brown. At this point, put on your rubber gloves and give the meat a gentle squeeze. You should feel it give beneath your fingers if it's done. Keep your rubber gloves on and transfer the meat from the grill to a cutting board. You should be able to lift off the skin with a few gentle tugs. Cut away any excess fat with a sharp knife. The remaining lean meat should be tender enough for you to easily tear off the bone and pull into shreds with your fingers (once it has cooled enough to handle!).

Put the pulled pork in a pan or bowl and splash it liberally with the following Lexington dip recipe (which I recommend) or a sauce of your choice. Toss the meat lightly in the sauce to ensure good coverage. Serve either on plates with sides of coleslaw and beans or on warm, soft buns topped with slaw.

BOB GARNER'S LEXINGTON-STYLE DIP

2 cups apple cider vinegar

1 cup water

⅔ cup brown or white sugar

½ cup ketchup

2 tablespoons Texas Pete

1 teaspoon salt

1 teaspoon pepper

1 teaspoon Worcestershire sauce

1 teaspoon onion powder

2 teaspoons Kitchen Bouquet browning sauce

Combine all ingredients in a large pot and bring to a simmer. Cook gently, stirring often, until sugar melts and flavors blend. Let sit for several hours before serving over chopped, sliced, or pulled pork shoulder. It's always a good idea to shake the sauce vigorously before using it.

FEATURE ATTRACTIONS

THE SKYLIGHT INN

Pete Jones stuck close to his hometown of Ayden, just south of Greenville, to tend the business he started in 1947, perhaps figuring that if his barbecue was good enough, the world would not only find the path to his door but turn it into a well-traveled road.

And that's basically what happened. National magazines and newspapers took notice of The Skylight Inn. People came from all over the world to sample the barbecue. VIPs wrote accolades on their autographed pictures.

Pete died in 2005. Nowadays, as his son Bruce looks after the restaurant's day-to-day operations, grandson Samuel often travels to barbecue-cooking demonstrations, regional food seminars, and other events, adding even more luster to the legacy Pete built by insisting on pit-cooking whole pigs over hardwood coals. The founder used to declare, "The old word is, 'The nose is the barb and the tail's the Q, and if you don't have the whole pig, you don't have barbecue.' " Pete didn't speak much French, but he gave some credence to the legend that the word *barbecue* came from the French *barbe à queue*, meaning "beard (or whiskers) to tail."

He also stoutly maintained that if it wasn't cooked over wood, it just wasn't barbecue. Today, both Bruce at the restaurant and Samuel on the road are doing as much as anyone in the country to spread that gospel. At The Skylight Inn, a little salt, vinegar, pepper, and Texas Pete, added as the 'cue is chopped, are all that's needed to bring out the perfection. The fatty stuff around the exterior surface of any pit-cooked pig absorbs most of the smoke and pit flavor, and some of that, chopped into the leaner pork, provides the defining characteristic of the 'cue at The Skylight Inn. I say it's best to moderate your general fat consumption, then let yourself experience some truly remarkable barbecue once in a while at a place like this.

The motto at Ayden's Skylight Inn is, "If it's not cooked with wood, it's not BBQ."

This is not a fancy restaurant. Expect to order either a barbecue sandwich with yellow coleslaw, or a "tray"—a stacked arrangement consisting of barbecue in a cardboard container, topped with a slab of flavorful baked cornbread, topped in turn with a cardboard container of coleslaw with a plastic fork sticking out of it. You'll still have one hand free to carry a drink from the counter to your table. The Skylight has soft-drink machines and iced-tea dispensers nowadays; for a long time, it offered only bottled soft drinks. Barbecued chicken, previously offered only at catered events, has been added on Thursday and Friday, and potato salad is now available. Whereas MoonPies and packaged fig cakes were the only dessert choices for years, slices of homemade cake are now for sale.

The Skylight Inn hasn't exactly seen a flurry of change over more than a half-century. Then again, this is a place where the idea of "cutting edge" is a barbecue cleaver. Let's hope it stays that way.

THE SKYLIGHT INN

4617 South Lee Street

Ayden, N.C. 28513

252-746-4113

www.skylightinnbbq.com

Lunch and dinner, Monday through Saturday

LEXINGTON BARBECUE

Wayne Monk, who founded Lexington Barbecue at its current location in 1962, still makes his presence felt around his famous restaurant, but his son Rick now runs the bustling, utterly traditional barbecue mecca.

There are several fine barbecue restaurants in Lexington, the town that is the spiritual center for one of North Carolina's two distinct barbecue styles. None of them, though, serves the region's signature wood-cooked pork shoulders as lean, moist, tender, yet firmly textured as you'll find at what locals call "the Monk" or "the Honey Monk," after the founder's nicknames.

If you want a treat normally reserved for insiders, order the "coarse-chopped outside brown," which is the chewy meat from the outside of the shoulder that absorbs most of the oak or hickory wood flavor. I'd advise you to get it in a paper tray, served with the local specialty, red or "barbecue" slaw. You'll marvel over the one-inch chunks of pit-cooked goodness, which, like all the restaurant's chopped and sliced barbecue, come to the table pre-sauced and perfectly moistened with mild, sweet Lexington dip, a thin hybrid combining the best flavors of the vinegar-pepper sauce of the east and the thicker tomato sauce of the Midwest and West.

This big, barn-like structure on U.S. 29/70 Bypass attracts more tourists and travelers from across the state and nation—well-read barbecue pilgrims, if you will—than any other joint in town. The city's other best ten or so barbecue places vie more for the loyalty of the locals. One competing Lexington restaurant—probably the locals' favorite, due to the relative absence of outsiders—switched to cooking with electric pits quite awhile ago, which is not nearly as socially acceptable in the Piedmont as in the coastal plain. Still, the expense and uncertain environmental regulation inherent in wood cooking are as real a concern in Lexington as anywhere, and Wayne Monk acknowledges that at some point in the future, all the town's restaurants may end up cooking some way other than directly over live wood coals.

Wayne and Rick tell me that as long as the decision is up to them, "we'll continue to cook and serve our barbecue the way we always have."

LEXINGTON BARBECUE

10 U.S. 29/U.S. 70 South

Lexington, N.C. 27295

336-249-9814

www.lexbbq.com

Lunch and dinner, Monday through Saturday

HILLSBOROUGH BBQ COMPANY

Co-owner Tommy Stann is adamant: "To me, the only way to have real North Carolina barbecue is to cook with wood. It just doesn't compare to pork that comes out of smokers and electric grills. So honestly, if the county hadn't let us do it, we just wouldn't have had a restaurant. It was either this way or no way, in our minds."

While its barbecue pits are traditional, Hillsborough BBQ Company took the unusual step of adding a bar and expanding into barbecue styles—beef brisket, pit-cooked ribs, barbecued chicken, and even turkey—heretofore more closely associated with other regions. "You know, we thought alcohol was important to help us grow, to maybe create more of a date-night atmosphere than might otherwise be the case, or so that you could have a draft beer with a barbecue sandwich," says Stann. "And we also thought that in a small town like this, we might get custom-

Hillsborough BBQ Company has an old-fashioned fireplace to burn wood down to coals, which are spread directly under the cooking meat.
UNC-TV

ers out more than one night a week if we had more than one meat. Nowadays, customers expect more, and that's why we have brisket, ribs, chicken, and turkey."

HILLSBOROUGH BBQ COMPANY

216 South Nash Street

Hillsborough, N.C. 27278

919-732-4647

http://hillsboroughbbq.com

Lunch, Tuesday through Sunday; dinner, Tuesday through Saturday

THE PIK-N-PIG

The Sheppard family was recruited several years ago to run a restaurant right beside the runway of the general aviation airport in Carthage. The unusual experiment has turned out well for the restaurateurs, the airport, pilots, locals, and foodies alike, since what has come to be known as The Pik-N-Pig is now the best barbecue restaurant in the Sandhills region.

This is not traditional North Carolina barbecue pit-cooked directly over live coals, but rather a tasty example of wood smoking. Most customers pronounce it delicious and don't quibble about the esoteric departure from traditional pit practices.

The Pik-N-Pig's smoker has an honest-to-goodness hickory wood fire in it. The meat, seasoned with a dry rub, is placed on rotating shelves that circulate through thick smoke and heat for up to twelve hours. Patrons rave about the wood-cooked flavor and tenderness of the Boston butts, smoked chicken, and sliced pork loin that are menu regulars, as well as the ribs featured on Saturday night.

The runway-side restaurant is a popular destination among central North Carolina pilots looking to log a few flight hours and enjoy an agreeable meal with other fliers. Pilots usually taxi up to the rustic restaurant a few minutes after landing, enlist passengers and customers to help them push their light aircraft

The Pik-N-Pig serves delicious, smoker-cooked barbecue to customers, many of whom fly their own planes to the Carthage airport that's home to the restaurant.
MIKE ONIFFREY

off the taxiway and onto the grass apron, then amble over to the dining room—or the open-air covered porch in fine weather—and place their orders. These almost always include slices of the homemade cakes or pies, all of which are outstanding, especially the chocolate cake topped with whipped cream.

The restaurant's answer to arguments over authentic pit cooking versus cooking in a smoker: "It isn't polite to talk with your mouth full."

THE PIK-N-PIG

194 Gilliam-McConnell Road
Carthage, N.C. 28327
910-947-7591
www.pik-n-pig.com
Lunch, Tuesday through Sunday; dinner, Tuesday through Saturday

SMITHFIELD'S CHICKEN 'N BAR-B-Q

Smithfield's chopped pork barbecue isn't pit-cooked over live coals, but it isn't prepared in a Western-style smoker either. It thus greets eastern North Carolina taste buds in a more familiar way than do other chain versions. Every Smithfield's location cooks its own pork shoulders on site, rather than having the meat trucked in from a central source. The barbecue is chopped to a not-too-fine consistency and appealingly seasoned. Topped with coleslaw, a Smithfield's barbecue sandwich provides an ideal flavor profile for this unique barbecue style. The portions are generous, and customers almost always award Smithfield's high marks.

SMITHFIELD'S CHICKEN 'N BAR-B-Q

Locations throughout North Carolina
scnbnc.com
Lunch and dinner daily

CONRAD & HINKLE PIMENTO CHEESE

Conrad & Hinkle normally makes around a thousand pounds of its famous pimento cheese each week, but the volume doubles during the holidays.
MIKE ONIFFREY

"OUT OF THIS WORLD."

"Best pimento cheese in the world."

"None better anywhere."

"Best pimento cheese ever."

Conrad & Hinkle's famous homemade pimento cheese gets overwhelmingly complimentary reviews, particularly for such a mild, middle-of-the-road version of the quintessential Southern delicacy. It uses mild American cheese, rather than the sharp cheddar preferred by many connoisseurs. One reviewer (seemingly in a tiny minority) opined, "Nothing to write home about . . . a little runny and too sweet . . . needs tightening up and some heat."

Now, that kind of comment—best made from the distance and relative anonymity of cyberspace—is enough to get a local resident deported from Lexington, the home of Conrad & Hinkle Grocery since 1919. The small, old-fashioned grocery near the town square has been making its signature pimento cheese from one of the founder's wife's recipes since 1940. It is the grocery's top-selling product. The store makes around a thousand pound per week—two thousand during the week before Christmas. Even when overall business at Conrad & Hinkle hits an occasional sluggish stretch, sales of pimento cheese remain constant. The product "got hot" during the 1980s. It's no secret that the pimento cheese's reputation probably kept Conrad & Hinkle's doors open during a time when consumers were drifting away from small, independent groceries and toward retail chain operations.

While pimento cheese gurus might disagree about whether or not Conrad & Hinkle's version stands out in any noteworthy way flavor-wise, nearly everyone acknowledges that the product has amassed an enviable reputation. "Nearly every restaurant, convenience store and chain grocery in the area carries Conrad & Hinkle pimento cheese and proudly displays signs saying so," wrote one local blogger. Customers regularly drive from Greensboro and High Point to stock up, and Lee Hinkle, grandson of cofounder Odell Hinkle, distributes the cheese spread to independent stores as distant as Charlotte. The product has also been shipped as far as Alaska and Germany. It's made fresh daily and will keep for four weeks in the refrigerator (if, as Lee Hinkle says, "you can go that long without eating it all"). The spread is sold in half-pound, one-pound, and two-pound containers. Individual customers often purchase ten or fifteen pounds at a time.

Something else no doubt enhances the popularity of Conrad & Hinkle's pimento cheese: local pride. Most everyone loves this mom-and-pop-style emporium, with its original stamped tin ceiling and concrete floors. The place is not only a favorite destination for local shoppers but also quite the tourist attraction. One of the front windows features a mural of the town and surrounding area, pointing out the locations of other local landmarks, such as the Bob Timberlake Gallery, some of the best-known barbecue joints, and Childress Vineyards.

Meats are still cut to order here. One older customer, who said he's been coming to Conrad & Hinkle since he was a little boy, pointed out, "It's the only place where you can still find bone-in chuck roast." The store makes its own link sausage, orders special hams and turkeys at Thanksgiving, and prepares fruit baskets at Christmas. It carries top-quality produce; Moravian chicken pies (see the Moravian Cooking chapter, pages 129-37); banana, strawberry, and rice puddings; homemade chicken, ham, and egg salads; homemade liver pudding; one of the largest barbecue sauce collections in the area; and jelly beans and other specialty candies.

Conrad & Hinkle also offers a couple of other essential products: a refined dedication to personal service and a warm environment with a pronounced family feeling. No wonder the pimento cheese has become such a hit.

CONRAD & HINKLE

6 North Main Street
Lexington, N.C. 27292
336-248-2341
www.conrad-hinkle.com

Brunswick STEW

Brunswick stew used to be a barbecue restaurant staple, particularly in eastern North Carolina. But the quality of the stew in several otherwise well-regarded eastern barbecue joints has declined markedly in recent years. I won't mention specifics, but eateries in the towns of Wilson, Rocky Mount, and Goldsboro come immediately to mind. On the other hand, some relatively new barbecue restaurants, particularly in Raleigh and Durham, have embraced a commitment to authentic, tasty Brunswick stew.

But Brunswick stew has never found its highest expression in restaurants anyhow. It has always been best known as a rural, community project. Of all the evocative traditional foods in North Carolina, Brunswick stew calls to mind the most vivid mental images of people sharing not only the ingredients and the task and fellowship of cooking but also the end product—a delicious meal. "Cooking a stew" is still an important ritual, both as a social event and a means of raising funds for local entities ranging from churches to rural fire departments.

People across the North Carolina countryside, especially those who do the cooking, are exceptionally set in their ways when it comes to Brunswick stew. Personal and family recipes, often handed down from one generation to another, are defended with great stubbornness and vehemence against any potential changes or competing claims of superiority.

Brunswick stew was originally cooked for upwards of ten hours in cast-iron pots over wood fires. Over the decades, it was stirred by generations of youngsters dragging wooden paddles in endless figure-eight patterns through the thick concoction, thereby giving themselves aching upper arms and shoulders. But the pain of stirring always paled in comparison to the potential consequences of not stirring sufficiently, thereby "sticking the stew," and the elder overseers of the process were always stern and unyielding in their admonitions. Smoke from the hardwood fires infused not only the clothing of the cooks but the contents of the pot, producing unmistakable evidence of hard labor. Today, when most rural Brunswick stew is cooked in aluminum

or stainless-steel pots over gas burners, some cooks' addition of bottled Liquid Smoke as a well-intentioned reminder of the former tradition is a patently inauthentic and, in my opinion, sad development.

Here in North Carolina, Brunswick stew has long been enjoyed most frequently as an accompaniment to pit-cooked barbecue. That isn't simply because they go so well together, although they certainly do, but rather because each was traditionally, albeit separately, prepared on all sorts of special occasions. Those attending the events would end up with a serving of barbecue on their plates, and a serving of Brunswick stew would inevitably come to rest on that same plate. Over time, the tastes of the two became associated with one another, most particularly in the northeastern quadrant of the state. Since barbecue is another of our iconic foods typically prepared in communal fashion, Brunswick stew and barbecue have a natural affinity, sharing the spotlight at community fund-raising events and in barbecue eateries alike. Residents of northeastern North Carolina normally don't think of barbecue without imagining stew to accompany it.

Brunswick stew is closely related to the mysterious ragout known as "burgoo," prepared only in Kentucky. But whereas burgoo is perhaps more concept than recipe, authentic Brunswick stew stays pretty close to a commonly accepted list of ingredients. South Carolina's pork "hash," normally served over rice, is another close cousin of Brunswick stew. Both burgoo and South Carolina hash—like our stew—are commonly served alongside barbecue, although burgoo is likely to sit next to a hunk of lamb or mutton barbecue, rather than pit-cooked pork.

Dishes combining meats and grains have existed for hundreds of years in both the Americas and Europe. Native Americans often stewed hominy and game in the same pot or cooked venison or bear with kernels of corn or pieces of squash. Surprisingly, visitors to the Tuscany region of Italy recount being served dishes that looked and tasted exactly like Brunswick stew and learning that those dishes dated back to the tenth century.

Forerunner dishes notwithstanding, various towns and counties bearing the name Brunswick claim to have invented this stew. The name Brunswick itself comes from Braunschweig, the ancestral German home of King George II of England, who awarded land grants to American colonists. Two Brunswicks most vigorously lay claim to the origin of Brunswick stew: Brunswick County, Virginia, just north of Warren County and the North Carolina line, and the coastal town of Brunswick, Georgia. Most scholars seem to think the more convincing case comes from Virginia.

There are two different accounts of the invention of Brunswick stew in Virginia. Both

Brunswick stew has traditionally accompanied barbecue, especially in eastern North Carolina, because both were prepared to celebrate special occasions.
JOHN BARNES

involve a Dr. Creed Haskins and an African-American cook named Jimmy Matthews, and both are set around 1828. According to one version, Dr. Haskins took his regular cook, Matthews, along to prepare the evening meal for an overnight hunting expedition. Matthews had planned to serve venison, the story goes, but the meat spoiled, so he improvised a stew containing squirrel, onions, butter, and stale bread (for thickening). In the other version of the tale, Matthews cooked up the stew to feed attendees at a political rally on the banks of the Nottoway River in Brunswick County.

Roy Blount Jr., the Georgia humorist, has been quoted as saying that "Brunswick stew is what happens when small mammals carrying ears of corn fall into barbecue pits." The earliest claims of Brunswick stew supposedly being prepared in Georgia came in 1898, which is when coastal Georgians say the dish originated. On display in the city of Brunswick is a twenty-five-gallon cast-iron pot bearing a plaque identifying it as the very vessel in which the dish was first cooked on nearby Sea Island.

Virginia probably gets the nod on the origin of the stew, but generations of "stew dogs" in Georgia, Virginia, and North Carolina have all developed great enthusiasm for the thick reddish orange dish. The constant, full-scale public-relations and publicity efforts in both Brunswick County, Virginia, and Brunswick, Georgia, are aimed at polishing their areas' culinary claims as a way of boosting tourism and economic growth. Virginia even went so far as to have its 1988 legislature pass a resolution proclaiming Brunswick County "the original home of Brunswick stew." Virginians claim that their invention migrated southward to North Carolina and Georgia. In support of the claim, they point out that the county seat of Brunswick County, Lawrenceville, is situated conveniently between Interstates 95 and 85, which, they say, helps the spread of Brunswick stew's popularity, allowing visiting motorists to carry locally cooked quarts of the stuff to parts near and far.

In the most traditional Brunswick stew recipes, the commonly accepted ingredients are tomatoes, butter beans, corn, potatoes, and onions, plus seasonings. The official Stewmaster's Association of Brunswick County, Virginia, says that a true recipe must contain chicken, with two possible additions. Competitive Brunswick stew cooking has a "Special" category, in which an entry can contain the standard ingredients plus beef. A "Deluxe" entry must contain the standard ingredients plus squirrel. No pork is allowed in any officially sanctioned "original" version of Brunswick stew in that corner of the Old Dominion.

Conversely, the original Georgia version of the stew is said to have begun with the cooking down of hogs' heads and organ meats. The Brunswick Golden Isles Convention and Visitors Bureau's recipe calls for the inclusion of chicken, pork, and beef, along with the standard vegetables and seasonings, plus some extra seasonings intended to replicate the flavor of the cooked-down hogs' heads. (South Carolina hash was also originally made with hogs' heads and organ meats; organ meats are no longer commonly used.)

All these traditions have, of course, gotten tangled up over the years. Brunswick stews through the southeastern United States may contain chicken, pork, beef, and the occasional squirrel or rabbit, as well as some wide-ranging additions to the standard vegetables and seasonings. One cook will add oatmeal for thickening, another might include crushed saltine crackers, and a third could stir in finely grated cabbage, meant to cook down to become part of the indistinguishable, thickened "base" of the stew.

Particularly in the Piedmont region, all sorts of extraneous ingredients—okra, sweet potatoes, green peas, squash, even green beans—are likely to be added to the basic ones. To an eastern North Carolinian, those ingredients represent creeping heresy. However, I have come to realize that if the extra vegetables are sufficiently cooked down to mush, so as to become impossible to identify individually, they do not detract from the stew but rather enhance its richness of flavor. From a traditional point of view, the only vegetables a cook wants visually identified in his or her stew are the ones I've already listed: tomatoes, butter beans, corn, potatoes, and onions. The visible presence of green beans, black-eyed peas, white beans, or carrots is a definite sign of inauthenticity to most die-hard Brunswick stew aficionados. Part of the decline of the Brunswick stew at some of the better-known barbecue joints has resulted from the practice of transforming the stew into a dish in which leftovers are routinely used up—and that often includes not only vegetables but also left-over barbecued pork, barbecued chicken, and who knows what else.

Strange ingredients can show up in the best-known Brunswick stews. The annual Mallard Creek Church barbecue near Charlotte is a huge fund-raiser for the church and a must-attend campaigning opportunity for any potential aspirant to public office in the Charlotte–Mecklenburg County area. The barbecue and the Brunswick stew are both highly regarded. However, it turns out that for years, the cooks have been putting rice in the Brunswick stew at Mallard Creek, which is practically unheard of elsewhere around North Carolina. Now, I have attended this event several times and have never noticed any evidence of rice in the stew, which leads me to conclude that, like other extraneous and often unidentified elements, the rice cooks down to a pasty consistency and becomes basically a thickener, helping form the baseline "stock" that provides the foundation for the tastes of the meat, vegetables, and seasonings.

Aside from a few die-hards, not too many people care about the individual ingredients of Brunswick stew. Most folks concentrate on the overall effect. No matter how the preparations vary from one spot to the next, there is a palpable reassurance and sense of continuity in partaking of something that has been prepared the same way, at least in particular locales, over several generations. Brunswick stew practically symbolizes working and socializing together, and for that reason alone, it remains one of our most cherished comfort foods.

BOB GARNER'S BRUNSWICK STEW

2 quarts water

1 chicken (about 3½ pounds), cut up

15-ounce can baby lima beans, undrained

8-ounce can baby lima beans, undrained

28-ounce can whole tomatoes, undrained, chopped

16-ounce package frozen baby lima beans

3 medium potatoes, peeled and diced

1 large yellow onion, diced

2 15-ounce cans cream-style corn

¼ cup sugar

¼ cup unsalted butter or margarine

1 tablespoon salt

1 teaspoon pepper

1 teaspoon hot sauce

Bring water and chicken to a boil in a Dutch oven. Reduce heat and simmer for about 40 minutes until tender. Remove chicken and set aside. Reserve 3 cups broth in Dutch oven. Pour canned lima bean liquid through a wire-mesh strainer into Dutch oven. Reserve beans. Add tomatoes and their liquid to Dutch oven and bring to a boil over medium-high heat. Cook, stirring often, for about 40 minutes until liquid is reduced by ⅓. Skin, bone, and shred chicken. Mash reserved beans with a potato masher. Add chicken, mashed and frozen beans, potatoes, and onions to Dutch oven. Cook over low heat, stirring often, for 3½ hours. Stir in corn and remaining ingredients. Cook over low heat, stirring often to prevent sticking, for 1 additional hour.

This stew was featured in *Southern Living* and on the Food Network's *Food Nation with Bobby Flay*. The recipe yields about 3½ quarts. The total cooking time is around 6 hours.

FEATURE ATTRACTIONS

THE PIT AUTHENTIC BARBECUE

At The Pit Authentic Barbecue's location in Durham, Brunswick stew is featured prominently at the very center of the dinner menu as "a savory, traditional accompaniment to North Carolina barbecue for nearly 200 years." When the second of The Pit's restaurants opened in November 2013, management decided to serve Brunswick stew in a twelve-ounce miniature cast-iron kettle so it would not only stay warm at the table but also remind guests of its historical importance in North Carolina's foodways. The stew is part of a "sharing menu" of meats and side dishes, each sized to serve two persons. The idea is that parties of four or more can order several different items and pass them around for a communal dining experience. "Cooking and eating Brunswick stew in North Carolina has always been all about sharing, and we want to encourage our guests to share it here, too," says The Pit's chef, Michael Lindsey.

Owner Greg Hatem grew up eating Brunswick stew alongside whole-hog barbecue in his hometown of Roanoke Rapids. But

The Pit's Brunswick stew, as served in both Durham and Raleigh, is in the bull's-eye of the flavor mainstream for eastern and central North Carolina. It contains all the traditional ingredients: stewed chicken and a complex chicken stock, tomatoes, butter beans, creamed corn, potatoes, onions, spices, and a satisfying dash of sugar to add the slight sweetness prized in much of the coastal plain. It's one of the best served by any restaurant in North Carolina.

THE PIT AUTHENTIC BARBECUE

321 West Geer Street

Durham, N.C. 27701

919-282-3748

thepit-durham.com

Lunch and dinner daily

328 West Davie Street

Raleigh, N.C. 27601

919-890-4500

thepit-raleigh.com

Lunch and dinner daily

ALLEN & SON BAR-B-Q

The Brunswick stew cooked up at Keith Allen's iconic barbecue restaurant between Chapel Hill and Hillsborough is some of the best I've encountered anywhere in the North Carolina Piedmont. That's probably because it's based on his grandmother's recipe and because it cooks long enough for the ingredients to really blend well and acquire the proper thickness.

During a visit to relatives in Roanoke Rapids, Dr. George Hatem helped cook the large pot of Brunswick stew he had requested.
HATEM FAMILY PHOTO

he also has another, rather unique inspiration for his restaurant's Brunswick stew. He likes to tell the story of his famous uncle, Dr. George Hatem, who led public health efforts in China for more than fifty years—and reportedly missed this particular North Carolina dish during the entire half-century. Dr. Hatem, known as Ma Haide in China, once requested during a visit to Roanoke Rapids that a pot of Brunswick stew be prepared and, furthermore, that he be allowed to stir it as it cooked.

In the coastal plain, beef is not a traditional meat in Brunswick stew, but in Allen's version (as in Brunswick County, Virginia), it is an entirely acceptable addition to the chicken, butterbeans, tomatoes, corn, potatoes, onions, and seasonings. (Some say, in fact, that Brunswick stew should contain two meats in order to be worthy of the name.)

"What we serve here is almost exactly the same stew I've cooked and eaten all my life, beginning when I learned the process from my grandmother," Allen says. "Brunswick stew was one of the ways folks in the country canned or 'put up' vegetables and meats for the winter, and it started in the late summer when everyone's gardens were running over, espe-cially with tomatoes and butter beans."

Squirrel and rabbit, added to the stew even as recently as Allen's childhood years, are no longer included in his restaurant's recipe. Of his Brunswick stew, Allen says one should be able to "hook it over a saltine cracker with a fork," which he recalls seeing his grandfather do on many occasions. It's terrific stuff.

ALLEN & SON BAR-B-Q
6203 Millhouse Road (at N.C. 86)
Chapel Hill, N.C. 27516
919-942-7576
Lunch, Tuesday through Saturday; dinner, Thursday through Saturday

At Allen & Son Bar-B-Q in Chapel Hill, Keith Allen serves basically the same Brunswick stew recipe he learned from his grandparents.
JOHN BARNES

ANNE'S OLD FASHIONED FLAT DUMPLINGS

CHICKEN PASTRY? Chicken and pastry? Chicken dumplings? Chicken and dumplings? Chicken slick?

No matter what you call it, it's a Southern staple, it's comfort food, and it's often served for Sunday dinner, to the delight of most.

It isn't a difficult dish to make, but when you start absolutely from scratch, it mandates a pretty big clean-up in your kitchen. Here's how one fellow remembers his mother making chicken pastry: "I can still see her spreading flour across our kitchen table and rolling out her dough into one big sheet that seemed to almost cover the entire table. Then she'd take a knife and make quick work of slicing it up into big squares while the chicken stock, along with that old hen, boiled away on the electric stove right behind her."

The typical instructions for the process? Flour the countertop. Throw the dough ball on the countertop and start rolling with a rolling pin. Roll out the dough nice and flat. Make sure enough flour is on it to keep it from sticking to the rolling pin. Roll and roll, making the dough round. Go side to side and back and forth until you have something like a pizza shape. Roll some more and add flour as needed to keep it from sticking. Feel the edges to be sure it's getting thin enough.

Do I hear some overwhelmed voices saying, "Forget it"?

Anne Briley Grimes really appreciates chicken pastry, which is what she says the dish is most often called when it's prepared in her home region of eastern North Carolina. She thinks people will serve it more often if they don't have to clean up after all that

flouring and rolling and adding more flour and more rolling. Thus, they'll have more time with the family to actually enjoy the dish, and less time away from the family while cleaning up pasty goo and loose flour from the countertop or table.

Making chicken pastry easier was the concept behind the founding of Harvest Time Foods in a converted carport in Greenville in

Anne Briley Grimes feels people will be more willing to prepare chicken pastry if they don't have to clean up a mess after rolling out homemade pastry.

1981. Mission: the marketing of packaged frozen dough strips. Customers were immediately receptive to the convenience of premade pastry. The product sold well in supermarkets from the beginning, with word of mouth moving things along at a faster-than-expected clip. Soon, letters asking for the product arrived from areas to the west, where people might call chicken pastry "chicken stew," "chicken and dumplings," or "pot pie." Harvest Time's distribution now covers most states east of the Mississippi and some farther west.

The company began sharing reviews like this one: "I tried these dumplings while visiting in Maryland during Thanksgiving. They have to cook a little longer [than homemade dumplings] but they are excellent." Another user, whose mother had made her own dumplings for decades, wrote, "Anne's Dumplings and those flat pastry strips became a part of our family, and like Colonel Sanders, they showed up more and more at our yearly family reunion dinners. Anne's makes a great pastry."

During the period of rapid market expansion, finding a name that would be recognizable to customers in various regions was a major challenge. "Anne's Dumplings for Chicken (Thin Pastry Strips)" worked well enough for a while, but ultimately, as the market grew geographically, "Anne's Old Fashioned Flat Dumplings (Thin Pastry Strips)" emerged as the most appropriate and descriptive name. The company developed new recipes to create other suggested uses for the dough product, such as lasagna, ravioli, casseroles, baked crackers, and fried, sugared pastry for desserts. In a nod to emerging health consciousness, Anne's began developing and marketing organic and whole-wheat flat dumpling strips, and also started planning for gluten-free flat dumpling strips made from rice. An original product—Anne's Chicken Base, which contained MSG—received a second look, leading to the development of five new bases in paste form that contain no MSG: Anne's Natural Chicken, Beef, and Ham; Anne's Organic Chicken; and Anne's Organic Vegetable.

Other new products are also gaining traction. Anne's "The One" sauce—dark, sweet, and peppery—is ideal as a marinade for grilling, roasting, or broiling meats. Anne's "The One" dressing is a tangy condiment intended for preparing coleslaw, egg salad, potato salad, and deviled eggs, in addition to being a salad dressing.

In 1992, the Small Business Association of North Carolina recognized Anne's as that year's "Small Business for North Carolina," and the national SBA awarded Anne's the Region IV Small Business of the Year Award.

The company's manufacturing facility has been located outside Ayden since 1990 and has been expanded numerous times.

Successfully marketing any food product is an achievement. Doing so while helping maintain a special regional food tradition and providing convenience is another, and that is Anne's greatest source of pride.

ANNE'S OLD FASHIONED FOOD PRODUCTS

Harvest Time Foods, Inc.

P.O. Box 98

Ayden, N.C. 28513

252-746-3160

www.annesdumplings.com

Banana Pudding
AND
PEACH COBBLER

Sure, banana pudding and peach cobbler have long been popular throughout the South, but they really do have a unique connection to North Carolina, in that they hold a revered place in our storied barbecue heritage.

Just picture any truly memorable barbecue and try to imagine it without one or both of these desserts as the quintessential finishing touch. Loyalties are split between the whole-hog, vinegar-kissed barbecue of the east and the milder, sweeter barbecue of the Piedmont and foothills. And the respective regions have different barbecue sides, including creamy versus peppery coleslaw. But from both sides of the state's longstanding east-west barbecue schism, generations of pit-cooked pork enthusiasts have made it clear that banana pudding and peach cobbler are their desserts of choice.

The reasons range from the practical to the sensory. Busy restaurants can turn out pans of either dessert quickly, and even the highest-quality recipes are relatively inexpensive to produce. There's also the consideration that creamy, smooth banana pudding helps soothe palates that may have been overstimulated, let us say, by immodestly spiced barbecue. But the best reason of all may be that finishing off the ritual meal with specific desserts gives us one additional tradition in a long list.

Bananas may be America's most consumed fruit, since they are imported year-round and delivered to practically every grocery. But there is no question about banana pudding's Southern bona fides.

The Chapel Hill–born rock band Southern Culture on the Skids has recorded songs about both banana pudding and fried chicken. In fact, its three members are fond of throwing both foods onto and into the crowd during performances. I once watched a video of assistants throwing whole buckets of banana pudding into an inflatable bouncy house full of the band's fans, who jumped, slithered, and danced with abandon to the tune. The lyrics of "Banana

Banana pudding—a beloved accompaniment to spicy North Carolina barbecue—soothes taste buds with its creamy texture.
UNC-TV

Puddin' " celebrate "day old and bold" banana pudding, "something funky with the skin on top."

So banana pudding is apparently a metaphor for sex and rock 'n' roll, if not necessarily drugs. Who knew? It isn't surprising, I guess, that a rapper named Alah Adams has written a novel entitled *Banana Pudding*, the first in a series of seven such novels Adams himself has christened a new genre, "hip hop lit." The main character is a beautiful stripper nicknamed Banana Pudding. One version of the book's dust jacket pictures her in a tight, custard yellow dress. "Never before has an author written such a unique interpretation of love, power and allure," says a promotional blurb about the novel. Whew!

Charlotte Observer food editor Kathleen Purvis has explored the mysteries of how banana pudding—the dessert—got to the South and why it largely stayed here, although there are other "puddin' pockets" around the country. In a 2010 *Charlotte Observer/News & Observer* article, Purvis explained that bananas were not generally marketed in the United States until the late 1800s, despite having arrived in the Caribbean from Africa in the sixteenth century. Cultivation of the fruit soon spread throughout Central America.

Bananas being unloaded in the port of New Orleans proved such an interesting spectacle that it became a tourist attraction, according to Purvis. Not long afterward, recipes for banana pudding began showing up in Southern cookbooks. In the early 1900s, Nabisco started marketing vanilla wafers, providing the last necessary link for the particularly Southern version of the venerable

English trifle, which contains fruit, custard, some form of cake or "sponge," and sweetened whipped cream. It is uncertain who dreamed up the idea of layering the plain wafers into the recently created dessert to form the sponge, but the fact that Nabisco soon began printing a recipe for banana pudding on its vanilla wafer boxes indicates the concept probably flowered in a short time.

Purvis's research also turned up the odd fact that 70 percent of America's bananas were once shipped by rail to Fulton, Kentucky, for subsequent distribution all over the country. Fulton began calling itself "the Banana Capital of the World" and was the site of the first banana pudding festival in the United States.

Today, the National Banana Pudding Festival is held annually in another random Southern town—Centerville, Tennessee. Although the festival promotes banana pudding as "America's favorite comfort food," and although attendees can sample the best among traditional recipes from fund-raising booths run by local nonprofits, the centerpiece is a cookoff in which contestants try to win prizes for new and different banana pudding recipes. Maybe it's just me, but as a lover of traditional Southern foods, the idea of constantly changing the recipe of something that's already so widely embraced doesn't present as the most comforting of concepts.

There are apparently no recipes approximating banana pudding anywhere in Latin America, although Cuba has a form of sweetened, mashed banana pie called "banana torte." So we know the recipe and tradition were not imported along with the bananas from farther south. Our regional variation of the dessert is hit-and-miss in terms of wide availability around the United States. So what, if anything, makes banana pudding Southern, other than its niche role as a North Carolina barbecue dessert? Maybe it's simply that it helps soothe the South's generally fevered brow, or cools the overall sultriness of life below the Mason-Dixon line.

There is no escaping the gritty reality that most North Carolina barbecue joints now make their banana pudding using instant vanilla- or banana-flavored pudding, rather than real egg custard or pastry crème (the difference being that pastry crème generally employs cornstarch as a thickener, whereas custard generally uses either no thickener or flour). If I'm totally honest, I'll have to say that the cooked variety of Jell-O vanilla pudding can make a respectable version of the classic dessert, while instant pudding doesn't produce a taste that's even close to being as good as the one obtained with cooked pudding.

I once conducted a church fellowship hall side-by-side comparison of various batches of banana pudding I had prepared at home. In one, I used the classic egg-yolk custard recipe that follows, while the other was prepared using Jell-O brand vanilla pudding, cooked according to package directions on the stovetop. The richer egg custard overwhelmingly carried the evening, but most everyone was surprised that the two were much closer in flavor and consistency than they expected. (Everyone also seemed quite willing to take home servings of the leftover Jell-O pudding version, which was also quite revealing.)

Still, my overriding reason for using an egg custard is that it doesn't make sense to me to separate egg whites for a meringue with which to top the banana pudding, then use vanilla pudding to make a custard substitute, rather than simply using the yolks from the eggs I just separated. Plus, the egg custard thickens more quickly than does the Jell-O vanilla pudding version.

Some may find the idea of making egg custard from scratch too intimidating. That might be especially true for those planning to use whipped cream, rather than a browned egg-white meringue, as a topping. For those situations, I suggest preparing Kraft Minute Tapioca according to the box directions (which actually include adding egg yolks). The tapioca produces a really tasty banana pudding custard, and I've gotten outstanding reviews when I've served this variation in large batches at pig pickings. Yet for the deepest flavor and a rich, golden color, it's hard to beat the egg-yolk version, particularly if you're going to make a meringue and will be separating the eggs anyhow. Just go with the flow here.

When neither the barbecue seasoning nor the seasonal temperature is near the top of the scale, peach cobbler is without question North Carolina's "other" barbecue dessert of choice.

Pie (or "pye") was the forerunner, of course. Cobblers were the inventive American twist to the old English custom, born during the Middle Ages, of pies prepared to hold both sweet and savory fillings. Featuring the fruits and berries of the new continent, which had been enjoyed by the native inhabitants for

centuries, cobblers could be prepared with a fraction of the flour it took to bake a loaf of bread. When first developed, they were usually prepared as a main dish for breakfast or lunch. It wasn't until the late nineteenth century that they began to find their present-day niche and became regarded mainly as desserts.

No one is sure where the name *cobbler* came from. It could hark back to the fourteenth century, referring to a wooden bowl. Or it could have been descriptive in origin, arising from the cobbler's biscuit-dough topping having a dimpled, "cobbled" appearance, not unlike the uneven surface of the cobblestones used to pave streets.

Since they often lacked brick baking ovens, colonial cooks improvised in their new surroundings by learning to make cobblers in pots over open fires. Later, during the nineteenth century, variations of the Dutch oven—a heavy, cast-iron, lidded vessel—were manufactured. They featured not only three legs to hold the round pot several inches over a bed of hardwood coals, but also a recessed top with a lip around the edge that would hold a second layer of live coals above the food cooking inside the pot. Cooks were thus able to more easily brown a cobbler's crust, which consisted basically of sweetened biscuit dough dropped or spread evenly atop boiling fruit.

During the short span of the cattle drives in the American West, cobblers made with fresh or dried fruit (and lots of sugar) were a welcome addition to the trail diet of cowboys, which consisted mainly of pork belly, beans, and beef. (Veteran chuck-wagon cooks also knew cobblers were an effective cure for

At Stamey's Barbecue in Greensboro, peach cobbler comes with soft-serve ice cream.
JOHN BARNES

the hangovers resulting from cowhands' periodic stopovers in trail towns.) Every good cook working with the cattle outfits had at least one cast-iron Dutch oven, invaluable in the preparation of not only cobblers but also the biscuits baked for practically every meal. At Western dude ranches, fruit cobblers are still a mainstay of the evocative "cowboy cuisine." They also form one important category in countless competitive Dutch oven cookoffs.

L. V. Anderson, who edits *Slate's* food and drink sections and writes a recipe column, "You're Doing It Wrong," got downright prickly when discussing cobbler terminology in a piece reprinted in the *News & Observer* in September 2013. One of Anderson's main beefs about cobblers was that cooks are too slack with their terms, willy-nilly interchanging *cobbler* with other variants. These include *buckle* (fruit filling poured on top of a thin cake batter, then baked until the batter rises above the fruit), *pandowdy* (fruit filling topped by a piecrust), and *crisp* (fruit filling topped by streusel consisting of brown sugar, flour, butter, and sometimes chopped nuts). Thankfully, she didn't get into the terms *slumps* and *grunts*, also used from time to time to refer to what were undoubtedly homely cousins to cobblers.

In North Carolina's Surry County, in the area immediately adjacent to Mount Airy, cobbler has long been known as *sonker* or *zonker*. These may be derivatives of a Scottish or Gaelic term meaning "to simmer." Like cobblers, sonkers are typically made with fruit fillings and various pastry or biscuit toppings, except in larger and deeper pans designed to feed more people. The most popular filling for sonker at Mount Airy's annual Sonker Festival (held the first Saturday of October) is reportedly sweet potato, served with a warm "dip" of milk, sugar, and vanilla.

But a proper cobbler, said Anderson, "is a dessert consisting of sugared (and often spiced) fruit topped with a sweetened biscuit topping and baked until the fruit is tender and the topping is golden."

Anderson continued with what came close to poetry: "The bottom part of the topping sinks into the fruit and sops up its flavorful juices, acquiring a dumpling-like texture; the top part undergoes the Maillard reaction [the chemical reaction that gives browned food its flavor] and gets brown and firm; the middle part arranges itself into a light, spongy crumb.

"Meanwhile, the rest of the fruit's juices mingle with the sugar and whatever thickener you've added to it (usually cornstarch or flour) to form a hot, sticky syrup that is best appreciated when juxtaposed with a scoop of vanilla ice cream. The cobbler is, in short, a tremendous dish."

Many Southerners remember summers when a fresh berry cobbler always seemed to be sitting on the back of the stove, waiting for family members to come along and help themselves to a serving. Whoever presided over the kitchen—Mother, Grandmother, or older sister—would simply gather whatever fresh fruit might be available, dump it in a pan with sugar and a little flour for thickening, and whip up a biscuit crust in nothing flat. This was never a fashionable or fancy dessert, but a beautifully browned cobbler was always

as inviting as it was homey, and that remains the case today.

The fact that you can also find cobblers at a great many of our best barbecue restaurants, where they join a veritable collage of food traditions, provides even more reason for celebration.

BOB GARNER'S PEACH PANDOWDY (OR COBBLER)

THIS COBBLER has a bright, fresh taste thanks to the lemon zest and lemon juice and doesn't seem overly sweet—which, in my opinion, makes it the perfect accompaniment to a smoky barbecue meal.

CRUST

3 cups flour
1½ teaspoons salt
2 sticks softened butter, cut into ½-inch slices
8 to 10 tablespoons ice water

FILLING

3 1-pound bags frozen, unsweetened peaches (or 7 cups sliced fresh peaches)
2 cups sugar
4 tablespoons flour
⅓ cup butter, melted
zest of 1 small lemon
juice of 1 small lemon

Sift flour and mix with salt. Using a pastry cutter, fork, or just your fingers, cut or work butter into flour until mixture is in even bits about the size of small peas. Gradually add ice water and mix lightly with a fork until mixture forms into a ball. Wrap in plastic wrap and chill in freezer for 5 minutes.

Thaw peaches, if frozen. In a mixing bowl, combine peaches, sugar, flour, melted butter, lemon zest, and lemon juice and mix thoroughly. Spread half of filling mixture in bottom of a 9-by-12-inch glass baking dish. Remove pastry from freezer and divide into 2 pieces. Roll or pat out to a normal piecrust thickness and cut into ½-inch strips. Lay strips across first layer of peaches. Roll out remaining pastry and cut it into strips. Pour remaining fruit into baking dish and lay remaining pastry strips atop fruit. Bake at 425 degrees for 10 minutes, then reduce heat to 350 degrees and bake an additional 50 minutes until golden brown. Cool and serve topped with vanilla ice cream or whipped cream.

If you prefer a more biscuit-like crust to make a proper cobbler, rather than pandowdy, substitute self-rising flour for the regular flour, add 4 tablespoons sugar to it, and eliminate the salt. Substitute 2 cups milk or buttermilk for ice water, but otherwise prepare the pastry the same way as described above.

If using biscuit topping, put all fruit filling into the pan at once (rather than in layers) and bake at 375 degrees for 20 to 25 minutes to partially cook filling. Remove hot filling from oven and drop biscuit dough by spoonfuls—and at regular intervals—over surface of filling, then use a rubber spatula to smooth it out as best you can. (Adding a little more milk or buttermilk to the dough will make it easier to drop by the spoonful.) The topping will rise and spread out as it bakes, even if you don't think it looks like enough crust. Return cobbler to oven and bake an additional 30 to 35 minutes until crust is golden brown. Serve warm with vanilla ice cream.

BILL SMITH'S BANANA PUDDING

BILL SMITH is the chef at the iconic Crook's Corner restaurant in Chapel Hill. This recipe is included in Smith's award-winning cookbook, *Seasoned in the South,* and was featured on American Public Media's *The Splendid Table.*

PUDDING
6 tablespoons cornstarch

4 cups half-and-half, divided

4 eggs

1 vanilla bean

1 cup sugar

stick of butter

1 box Nabisco Nilla Wafers

2½ pounds bananas (6 or 7 medium bananas)

MERINGUE
cider vinegar

salt

8 egg whites at room temperature

¼ teaspoon cream of tartar

1 cup sugar

2 teaspoons vanilla

Whisk cornstarch into 1 cup of the cold half-and-half, then whisk in the eggs until completely blended. Heat the other 3 cups of half-and-half with the vanilla bean until they begin to steam a little. Drizzle warm milk into eggs, stirring constantly. Cook mixture in a double boiler or a heavy-bottomed pot over medium heat until it begins to thicken enough to coat a spoon. Sometimes this happens quickly; sometimes it takes forever. Whisk in sugar and cook 1 or 2 minutes longer, but take care because custard will now scorch more easily. Remove vanilla bean and stir in butter in pieces. The butter will seem to thin the custard a little, but the effect is temporary. The butter must be completely absorbed. Pour a cup or so of the custard into a pretty, ovenproof serving bowl. Swirl it around to coat the bowl. Line bowl with vanilla wafers, then fill bowl by layering it with custard, cookies, and bananas. Let pudding settle.

Meanwhile, rinse a mixing bowl with vinegar and dust it with salt. Dump it out over the sink. What remains in the bowl will be the right amount. Put egg whites in bowl and begin mixing at low speed. Add cream of tartar and increase speed to medium. Feed in sugar slowly. Increase speed to almost maximum. Beat until meringue is fairly stiff. Bump speed up to maximum for a minute, then turn it back down to low and add vanilla. Mix well.

Spread meringue over top of pudding in dramatic swirls. Dust heavily with more sugar. Bake at 350 degrees for about 15 minutes until pretty and brown.

Crook's Corner in Chapel Hill
UNC-TV

FEATURE ATTRACTIONS

STAMEY'S OLD FASHIONED BARBECUE

The folks at Stamey's serve three outstanding cobblers—apple, cherry, and peach—but they say peach outsells the others by about ten to one. Peach cobbler topped with vanilla ice cream is such an institution at Stamey's that I once asked the late Keith Stamey, son of founder Warner Stamey, to make one for me to serve during an appearance on ABC's *Good Morning America*. When I came to pick it up, he told me he had started over four or five times before he ended up with a cobbler that he thought looked pretty enough for national TV. (Ironically, because the director cut the time of the live segment, that peach cobbler never got on the air!)

Since you'll be getting it by the serving, the appearance of the whole cobbler surely won't matter to you. You'll find the taste superb. Typically, Stamey's peach cobbler is topped with soft-serve ice cream.

Like those served at nearly all barbecue restaurants, the fruit cobblers at Stamey's feature a sweetened biscuit topping. Most restaurant versions also use canned peaches, which aren't as ideal as fresh or frozen, although the huge difference in cost makes this choice understandable. All I can say is that, as a grace note at the end of a memorable barbecue meal, Stamey's approach works beautifully.

Stamey's Old Fashioned Barbecue

STAMEY'S OLD FASHIONED BARBECUE

3206 High Point Road

Greensboro, N.C. 27403

336-299-9888

stameys.com

Lunch and dinner, Monday through Saturday

2812 Battleground Avenue (U.S. 220 North)

Greensboro, N.C. 27408

336-288-9275

Lunch and dinner, Monday through Saturday

HILL'S LEXINGTON BARBECUE

Founder Joe Allen Hill and his wife, Edna, put Hill's on the map in 1951 by being the first to use the term *Lexington barbecue* in honor of Hill's hometown, even though the new restaurant was in Winston-Salem. Gene Hill, Joe and Edna's son, and his wife, Sue, kept building the place's reputation for Lexington-style pork shoulder, served chopped, blocked (or pulled), and sliced, plus outstanding barbecued chicken and fish-camp-style seafood.

But one of Hill's biggest drawing cards is what is arguably the best banana pudding in North Carolina. Manager J. R. Hill, grandson

Hill's Lexington Barbecue
UNC-TV

Banana Pudding and Peach Cobbler | 99

of the founders, now oversees the preparation of this family tradition: a concoction of rich, old-fashioned egg custard topped with some of the most beautifully turned-out meringue you will ever see. (The top of a Hill's pan of banana pudding reminds me of the ocean, rolling in waves toward shore.) While it's true that even the worst banana pudding is pretty doggone good, what is reverently served to the pilgrims showing up at Hill's door on the north side of Winston-Salem puts to shame the many make-do restaurant versions thrown together with instant pudding.

HILL'S LEXINGTON BARBECUE

4005 North Patterson Avenue

Winston-Salem, N.C. 27105

336-767-2184

Breakfast, lunch, and dinner daily

AUNT RUBY'S PEANUTS

EASTERN NORTH CAROLINA, including Halifax County, is prime growing territory for Virginia-type peanuts, which are known for low fat content, meatiness, superior texture, and appealing flavor. These large peanuts are increasing in popularity, particularly for salting, for roasting in the shells, for frying, and for confections. They're sometimes called "the peanut of gourmets."

Which is where Aunt Ruby's comes in. A & B Milling Company was established in 1945 in the small town of Enfield as a feed, seed, and fertilizer store to serve local farmers. But since Halifax is one of the foremost of North Carolina's peanut-producing counties, it was a natural thing

Aunt Ruby's peanut products
A & B MILLING COMPANY

for the company to transition into the mail-order peanut business. Aunt Ruby's high-grade peanuts are shelled, processed, and distributed nationally from the local plant, as they have been for over half a century.

These memorable home-style peanuts are prepared and packaged in the following delicious forms: raw shelled, roasted in the shell, fried (country-style), and honey-roasted. Roasted redskin peanuts, chocolate-covered peanuts, and peanut brittle are other favorites. The company also processes shelled pistachios and (as of relatively recently) cashews and offers several gift combination packages.

Many non-locals who venture off I-95 to visit Aunt Ruby's (which offers free samples) are surprised to learn that peanuts don't grow on trees like pecans and walnuts, and even that they aren't nuts at all but legumes. Peanut plants are unusual in that they flower above ground, with the peanuts themselves growing under the ground.

The harvesting process is interesting. Peanuts are gathered in the fall, when they're pulled from the ground by harvesting machinery and turned over to dry in the field in the open air for several days. Then combines separate the still tender, moist peanuts from the vines and blow them into special hoppers. Next, they're dumped into a drying wagon, where forced warm air cures them. The peanuts are inspected and graded for sale at buying stations. Only the largest and most attractive specimens are selected for the whole-peanut market.

NORTH CAROLINA PEANUT PIE

CRUST

1½ cups unbleached all-purpose flour

1 teaspoon sugar

½ teaspoon salt

1 stick chilled unsalted butter, cut into ½-inch cubes

4 tablespoons or more ice water

FILLING

⅓ cup dark brown sugar, packed

2 tablespoons all-purpose flour

½ teaspoon coarse salt

¼ teaspoon ground cinnamon

¼ teaspoon cayenne pepper

3 large eggs

½ cup golden syrup (such as Lyle's)

½ cup sorghum syrup or ½ cup golden syrup mixed with 1 teaspoon apple cider vinegar

¼ cup unsalted butter, melted, then cooled slightly

1 teaspoon vanilla

1½ cups coarsely chopped salted North Carolina peanuts

vanilla ice cream

Blend flour, sugar, and salt in a food processor. Using on/off turns, cut in butter until mixture resembles coarse meal. Add 4 tablespoons ice water and blend, using on/off turns, just until moist clumps form. Add more ice water by teaspoonfuls if dough is dry. Gather dough into a ball, then flatten into a disk. Wrap in plastic and chill at least 1 hour.

Preheat oven to 375 degrees. Roll out dough on a lightly floured surface to a 12-inch round. Transfer to a 9-inch glass pie dish. Fold edges under and crimp decoratively. Freeze crust for 15 minutes.

Line crust with foil and fill with dried beans or pie weights. Bake about 20 minutes until crust is set. Remove foil and beans. Continue baking for about 13 minutes until edges begin to color, piercing with a fork if crust bubbles. Cool crust on a rack while making filling. Maintain oven temperature.

Combine brown sugar, flour, salt, cinnamon, and cayenne in a medium bowl. Whisk eggs in another medium bowl to blend. Add golden syrup, sorghum, melted butter, and vanilla to eggs and whisk to blend. Add brown sugar mixture and whisk until smooth. Mix in peanuts. Pour filling into cooled crust.

Bake pie for 15 minutes. Reduce temperature to 350 degrees and continue to bake about 40 minutes until crust is golden and filling is set (center may move slightly when pie dish is gently shaken); cover edges with foil if crust is browning too quickly. Cool pie on a rack; if preparing a day ahead, cover loosely and store at room temperature. Cut pie into wedges and serve with vanilla ice cream.

Note: Lyle's Golden Syrup can sometimes be found in the supermarket aisle with maple syrup and other syrups. It's also available at kitchenandcompany.com.

AUNT RUBY'S PEANUTS

A & B Milling Company

200 Halifax Street

Enfield, N.C. 27823

800-PEANUTS (732-6887) or 252-445-3161

www.auntrubyspeanuts.com

Collard GREENS
PROOF WE ARE LOVED

Southerners say collard greens are proof we are loved. And many of us love them right back:

> From age to age the South has hollered
> The praises of the toothsome collard.
> Our parents' precepts we have follered,
> And countless messes we have swallered.

A few years ago, students at the University of Mississippi sang these and other lyrics as part of an opera devoted to collards at the Southern Foodways Alliance's annual symposium in Oxford. That highfalutin musical undertaking was based on *Leaves of Greens: The Collard Poems*, published three decades ago by the Ayden Collard Festival in North Carolina. Ayden is also the hometown of Nicky Harris, a rock 'n' roll singer known for his sultry local performances of his composition "My Baby Loves Collard Greens," which is about as "get down" as music can possibly be, at quite the opposite end of the spectrum from opera.

The point is that, highbrow or hoi polloi, everybody loves collard greens, or at least loves the idea of loving collard greens.

A "mess" of the greens, simmered until tender in pork broth and maybe even shiny from an extra anointing of bacon drippings, is the bedrock of country cooking in North Carolina and elsewhere across the Southeast. But the rest of the world loves collard greens pretty well, too, it seems.

In Ethiopia, they're cooked in butter flavored with herbs and spices or steamed in olive oil with red onions, garlic, and green peppers in a dish called *gomen wat*, often found in Ethiopian restaurants in the United States. Portuguese green soup (*caldo verde*), containing chopped greens, potatoes, onions, and garlic, is something of a national dish, served almost daily. Elsewhere in the Mediterranean region, they're often sautéed with onions, garlic, and tomatoes. Collards are growing in popularity in the northeastern United States, where they're served raw as a salad green, as wraps for various savory fillings, or in soy-milk-based cream sauce.

Some say collards have been around so long they can be considered "the dinosaur of vegetables." They're a type of wild cabbage. Plants pretty much in their present-day form have existed for at least two millennia. The Anglo-Saxon *cole wort* or *colewyrt*, which simply means "cabbage plant," was gradually Anglicized to *collard*.

The ancient Greeks are said to have raised collards, although they disliked the flavor enough that they apparently consumed only the stems. The Romans reportedly considered collards potent detoxifying agents. Legend proclaims that Julius Caesar ate generous helpings of collard greens as a way of warding off indigestion after royal banquets. Some today claim that cruciferous vegetables such as cabbage, collards, kale (another collard cousin), and broccoli contain agents useful in fighting cancer.

By the first century A.D., collards made their way to Great Britain. They were not immensely popular and may have been tolerated mainly because they persevered during the winter months, when other vegetables wouldn't grow, as well as because of belief in their health benefits. Collards had a reputation for unsophistication, it seems. The strong odor produced by cooking them wasn't appreciated any more during the early centuries than it is today. The odor of collards simmering often greeted me when I entered my grandmother's home in Newport, North Carolina, as a child, and I still recoil from that odor more than sixty years later. Like most children, I didn't like collards. But like most Southern adults, I have since acquired a real taste for them.

We're not sure whether the Romans or the Celts brought collards to Britain, but we do know that the British later brought seeds to North America, although cultivated collards were in the Caribbean as early as 1565. By the time the first slaves arrived in Virginia in 1619, collards were already growing there. At first, the greens were considered food for poor folks, black and white. They hung on in the winter when no other vegetables would grow, and they could be flavored by scraps of pig meat such as the feet, tails, and skin, which otherwise would have been discarded. As slaves began working in the kitchens of Southern farms and plantations, they served collards at their masters' tables, and this "soul food" gradually became an iconic Southern favorite, loved by blacks and whites equally. Nowadays in many parts of the South, any big occasion calls for cooking up a pot of collards.

"In lots of families, you'll hear someone say, 'Mmm, we had collards, collards, collards,'" says Benny Cox, a collard grower and retailer from Ayden. "Now, there are some other families in which someone might sort of roll their eyes, come up with a slightly different inflection, and say, 'Humph, we had collards, collards, and more collards!' They're such a big part of everyday life around here that some people get a little carried away."

Though collard plants do well in the high heat and plentiful rainfall of the South, they're often harvested during cooler weather. Most connoisseurs think they achieve their peak flavor during autumn, winter, and spring, once cold temperatures have converted their starches to sugar and changed the structure of some of the proteins. Certain varieties tend to be tough and bitter during the summer months. But those same varieties are usually

Yellow cabbage collards are much lighter in color than the dark-green Georgia collards commonly found in grocery stores.
UNC-TV

transformed after the first frost, when cooking times can be significantly reduced and when the collards become sweet and velvety on the tongue.

Collards are harvested by priming—that is, by picking leaves off the stalks as they're needed. Some delicate varieties are damaged by frost, after which new transplants have to be set out, while others survive quite well during rough winter temperatures, their primed stalks putting out delicious, tender shoots in early spring. Although the greens can be grown anywhere in North Carolina, the distribution is uneven across the state. The real "collard belt" is in North Carolina's central coastal plain.

In most areas of North Carolina, and even in much of the central coastal plain, the majority of the greens available in stores and farmers' markets are dark green, loose-leaf varieties commonly called "Georgia collards." Many home gardeners use various "VATES" seed varieties, perhaps not realizing that the name is an acronym for the Virginia Truck Experiment Station, where these types were developed and improved.

The portion of the coastal plain around Pitt and Edgecombe counties is home to a particularly celebrated heirloom variety of the greens: yellow cabbage collards. Tending to "head up" at the top of the stalk in a shape resembling a cabbage, they look markedly different from the green Georgia collards sold elsewhere around the state, having a lighter green-to-yellowish cast. They taste different as well. Just about anyone who has ever tasted yellow cabbage collards says they are considerably more tender and yielding to the tooth than loose-leaf collards. They are sweeter than the Georgia varieties even during the summer months, with little or none of the bitterness the other greens typically possess during hot weather. Because the leaves are more tender, the collards cook quicker and do not have to be boiled into submission.

George Wooten, who lives near Pinetops, contracts with a farmer in Edgecombe County to grow the yellow cabbage collards he sells to area restaurants and supermarkets. Like most growers of this variety, he neither buys nor sells the seeds, which are not available in seed catalogs. In fact, Wooten's family has been growing yellow cabbage collards, harvesting the seeds, and passing them down for close to a hundred years.

Benny Cox of Pitt County sells most of the yellow cabbage collards he raises at the Collard Shack, located right beside the famous Skylight Inn barbecue restaurant in Ayden. Unlike most yellow cabbage collard producers, Cox does sell seeds and young plants, which he says will grow throughout the coastal plain (although he hints he keeps a few local growing secrets close to the vest). He and his wife, Vicki, also offer harvested collards at the Collard Shack, as well as cooked and seasoned frozen collards.

Actually, cooking and freezing extra yellow cabbage collards during periods when they're plentiful is standard procedure in this area. The "heading" collards don't tolerate extreme cold as well as do the loose-leaf Georgia collards, so they're often unavailable during February, March, and part of April. Residents of the yellow cabbage collard zone don't much like the idea of switching to the dark green, loose-leaf greens during those months, since they still take considerably longer to cook and aren't as sweet, even after the first frost. So several area restaurants and groceries began cooking vast quantities of the heirloom variety in late autumn and freezing them in quart containers, so they'll be able to supply their customers' holiday demands, as well as provide plenty of the tasty greens during the "blackout" period for the yellow cabbage variety.

For as long as anyone can remember, cooks in the South have known that the best way to cook collards—if emphatically not the healthiest way —is to start by putting some pork seasoning meat into several quarts of water and simmering it for at least an hour to make a flavorful broth. The meat can be ham hocks, pig feet, pig tails, hog jowls, other pork scraps, or ham bones. Once the broth is ready, the collard leaves are dropped into the liquid either relatively whole (to be chopped or shredded once they're tender) or torn into small pieces. Cookbook author and restaurateur Mildred Council of Chapel Hill, who's more popularly known as Mama Dip, tightly rolls collard leaves once she's trimmed them off the center stalk. She then cuts them crosswise into thin strips before putting them into the cooking liquid. Many cooks use a handheld, circular-collar chopper to further dice the greens once they're cooked and drained. Many folks add some red pepper pods to the broth along with the collard leaves, after which the collards need to be simmered until they're tender. It takes an hour or longer for most Georgia collards, depending on the season. Yellow cabbage collards are usually tender and ready to eat within thirty minutes.

One old-fashioned touch not seen much any longer is to drop some dumplings made of cornmeal, salt, and water into the collard "pot liquor" about fifteen minutes before the greens are done. Then the finished greens are drained, minced or shredded, and seasoned to taste with some or all of the following: sugar, vinegar, hot sauce, salt, pepper, and maybe a little bacon grease or cooking oil for "shine" and flavor.

More than a little folklore surrounds the consumption of collards. Nearly everyone in the South is familiar with the tradition that encourages the consumption of collards and black-eyed peas, accompanied if possible by hog jowls, on New Year's Day. Many regard pigs, and hog jowls specifically, as symbols of luck. The old superstition decrees that those eating collards and peas will make money during the new year. The greens symbolize folding money, while the peas represent the "jingle."

Benny Cox sells loose cabbage collards plus cabbage collard seeds and plants at the Collard Shack in Ayden.
UNC-TV

Author with a forkful of collard greens
MIKE ONIFFREY

Some people believe that hanging a collard leaf over the door guarantees good luck. Placing a collard leaf on the forehead of someone with a headache is thought by many to be a surefire way to chase away the pain. Iconic jazz pianist Thelonious Monk, a Rocky Mount native, sometimes wore a collard leaf pinned to his lapel when playing in New York City clubs. Monk joked he was thereby displaying his "sole" (and "soul") credential. More importantly, he was no doubt establishing a connection with his fans, many of whom had either made their living on the Southern soil or, like Monk, had generations of ancestors who did.

Particularly for middle-class North Carolinians over the age of fifty, an emotional connection to a simpler time and a slower,

subsistence-level agrarian lifestyle often helps fuel the fondness for traditional foods such as collard greens. Yet even as we yearn for the old ways, we know all too well that the style of cooking known to our parents and grandparents is too often loaded with fat and cholesterol. Those who have the resources to do so have largely adapted to a healthier diet brought about through societal awareness and pressure.

Collards are actually listed as one of "the World's Healthiest Foods" by nutritionist and biologist George Mateljan, although they certainly wouldn't be rated after being simmered in pork fat, Southern-style. Chefs and bloggers have come up with dozens of ways to braise them, dress them with olive oil and spices, cut down on or eliminate meat, and wrap them around other foods as they come up with their own contemporary takes on classic Southern dishes.

But plenty of us leave enough wiggle room in our diet strategies to work in occasional visits to the diners and meat-and-three restaurants serving traditionally cooked Southern foods. We enjoy batches of old-time, pork-accented collards during holidays and family reunions and church dinners. And we set aside some space in our lives for special events such as the annual Collard Festival in the Pitt County community of Ayden, which promotes itself as "the Collard Capital of the World." Along with the typical funnel cakes, rides, and parade, the festival features revelers dressed in collard leaves and the crowning of the Collard Queen (who is actually feted

as "Miss Ayden" these days). The September event is best known for its collard-cooking and collard-eating contests, the latter of which normally requires the winner to put down seven or eight pounds of collards at one sitting.

Of course, festival or no festival, a lot of collard eating is always going on at Bum's Restaurant on Third Street, recognizable by the little patch of collards planted out front. Owner Latham "Bum" Dennis grows in his own personal garden all the collards his restaurant serves. He's pretty much turned over the cooking to his son, Larry, who gets up most mornings to start a big pot of collards cooking long before daylight. Rather than making a broth first, Larry gets the collards simmering in water in one pot while he makes his stock,

Lots of ham goes into the collard seasoning stock at Bum's Restaurant in Ayden.

or dressing, in a second pot. He begins braising different types of ham for seasoning—fresh (uncured) ham, "tenderized" ham, country ham—and adds a secret mixture of sauces and seasonings. When all the flavors have blended to his satisfaction, he pours the buttery mixture over the cooked collards. Next, he puts the steaming collards—flavorful stems and all—through a chopping machine so they emerge minced very fine, puréed to nearly the consistency of creamed spinach. Ayden may have some of the planet's most discriminating collard enthusiasts, so it's revealing that Larry Dennis serves up to two hundred gallons of collards some weeks at Bum's.

Agricultural researchers point out a decline in the number of home collard patches in North Carolina. Some also claim that collard consumption is decreasing, especially among the young, although my own unscientific observation is that a great many young diners are enthusiastically eating collards in restaurants, since they're considered trendy these days.

Between the fondness for collards among middle-aged-and-up consumers, a new cachet for the greens among younger diners, and the increasing popularity of collards outside the South, the commercial market for the pungent greens is fairly steady. I personally believe consumption is holding strong in our state as well, although more collards are certainly eaten in restaurants than are grown and cooked at home nowadays. Indeed, there seems to be no decline whatsoever in the loyalty—even reverence, if you will—accorded these hardy and humble greens.

SOUTHERN COLLARD GREENS

1 pound collard greens
¼ pound pork fatback, rinsed well
    and cut into 1-inch cubes
1 yellow onion, sliced ¼-inch thick
2 medium carrots, sliced
1 ham hock
5 cups chicken broth
¼ cup cider vinegar
2 tablespoons Worcestershire sauce
2 tablespoons soy sauce
1 teaspoon dried thyme
½ teaspoon freshly ground pepper

Pick through collards and discard any old and discolored leaves. Strip leaves off stems by grasping the base in one hand and pulling leaves away from stems with the other. To clean collards, fill sink with cold water. Add collards and stir vigorously with your hand; let the dirt fall to bottom of sink. Let collards sit undisturbed for 1 to 2 minutes. Carefully remove collards from water and place in a colander. Rinse out sink and repeat washing process 2 more times. After the third cleaning, carefully lift collards out of the water, place in a salad spinner, and spin until dry.

Heat a large saucepan over medium-high heat. Add fatback and cook for 5 to 10 minutes until it renders some fat. Add onions, carrots, and ham hock and cook for 25 to 30 minutes until onions

Chef Jay Pierce at Lucky 32 Restaurant in
Greensboro stirs a batch of his signature
collard greens.
MIKE ONIFFREY

are a dark golden brown. Add greens to
pan and cook, stirring, until wilted. Add
broth, vinegar, Worcestershire sauce, soy
sauce, thyme, and pepper. Cover pot and
simmer for 45 minutes until greens are
tender.

This recipe serves 4. It comes from
Jay Pierce, chef at Lucky 32 Southern
Kitchen in Greensboro, courtesy of Diane
Daniel of Farm Fresh North Carolina.

FEATURE ATTRACTIONS

SMITH'S RED AND WHITE GROCERY AND RESTAURANT

Several expanded or new grocery stores
have been built on the same basic site since
founder Sherwood Smith began a grocery
business in a feed and fertilizer store in the
old Dortches schoolhouse near Rocky Mount
in 1954. But as newer, more modern facilities
have periodically arisen, the country atmosphere and heritage of the unusual complex
have remained unchanged.

Smith's is a sprawling, full-service grocery
store that even has an in-store bank now. But
it is particularly well known both to locals
and far-flung residents of the Southeast for
the excellence of its pork products and its
extensive selection of old-fashioned candies,
layer cakes, and succulent, perfectly seasoned
cooked collards.

The tiny community of Dortches is on
the outskirts of Rocky Mount just a mile or
so off I-95. Thousands of those in the know
make Dortches and Smith's a regular stop as
they travel the interstate. They often bring
along coolers to carry home twenty, thirty, or
forty pounds of Smith's incredibly popular
link sausage.

Smith's buys heirloom yellow cabbage
collards from Edgecombe County's George
Wooten. Knowing there will come a two-
to three-month period when killing frosts
will make fresh collards unavailable, Smith's

Smith's Red & White in Dortches sells cooked cabbage collards by the quart in the grocery and also serves the greens in the adjacent restaurant.
UNC-TV

begins cooking and packaging them by the quart as the holidays approach. A great many households in the area—and indeed across a wide swath of North Carolina and neighboring states—buy their cooked and seasoned collards for Thanksgiving and Christmas from Smith's. Customers can also be assured of obtaining the toothsome greens in frozen form during February, March, and April. Most folks find that the collards taste just as good, if not actually better, after having been frozen. They seem to get sweeter and more tender.

In 2010, Smith's opened a little gem of a home-cooking restaurant right beside the grocery store for customers who prefer to enjoy collards, sausage, country ham, barbecue, and other store specialties on site, or to get takeout plates.

SMITH'S RED AND WHITE GROCERY AND RESTAURANT

3635 North Halifax Road

Rocky Mount, N.C. 27804

252-443-0418 (restaurant); 252-443-4323 (store)

www.smithsredandwhite.com

Breakfast and lunch, Tuesday through Saturday

SHARPSBURG RESTAURANT

Collard grower George Wooten, certainly an authority, says this humble place in Rocky Mount wins his personal collard taste test among the restaurants he supplies with the greens.

The Sharpsburg Restaurant was something of an institution on U.S. 301 (Hathaway Boulevard) in Rocky Mount before a 2011 fire destroyed the former location. However, the restaurant reopened shortly thereafter at a nearby spot on N.C. 97, as owner Faye Logan decided not to throw in the towel. The customers have obviously followed.

In addition to collards, which usually are available from May through January, the restaurant is well known for its country buffet and as a great spot for morning victuals. One customer enthused, "Breakfast is absolutely the best meal of the day."

The Sharpsburg Restaurant in Rocky Mount is regarded as one of the best eateries for perfectly cooked and seasoned cabbage collards.

SHARPSBURG RESTAURANT

11792 N.C. 97 East

Rocky Mount, N.C. 27803

252-442-0789

Breakfast, Monday through Saturday; lunch and dinner, Monday through Friday

Pickles on the line at Mt. Olive Pickle Company

THE MT. OLIVE PICKLE Company still occupies its original location at the corner of Cucumber and Vine in tiny Mount Olive in Wayne County. The company traces its roots to the mid-1920s, when Shickrey Baddour, a Lebanese immigrant from Goldsboro, thought he recognized an opportunity in buying locally raised cucumbers, brining them, and selling them to pickle companies. He sought out the help of George Moore, a sailor from Wilmington who had worked in a Castle Hayne pickle plant.

It seemed like a terrific plan, but it didn't work because they had no buyers for their product. So Baddour and Moore set out to correct that small detail. And they did so, although not in the way they originally imagined.

By January 1926, they had recruited a group of thirty-seven local businesspeople as the original shareholders and investors in Mt. Olive Pickle Company. The company's new mission was to pack and sell its own pickles. It hired Moore as factory superintendent and Baddour as salesman and purchased one acre of land from farmer J. A. Westbrook for a thousand dollars. That small plot is still part of the company's manufacturing site today.

The first year, all the production was done by hand. The cucumbers were taken from brining vats to nearby tables, where the jars were packed. Old coffeepots were used to pour syrup into the jars.

Since those beginnings, Mt. Olive has grown into the second best-selling pickle brand in the country, at times ranking number one in unit sales. It is first by a significant margin in the Southeast and is the largest privately held pickle company in the United States. Sales growth into new markets continues apace.

Mt. Olive's broad product line includes sweet and bread-and-butter pickles, dill and sour pickles, kosher dill pickles, hot dill pickles, relishes and salad cubes, and practically a peck of pickled peppers.

If you want to experience the culture of the pickle, plan to celebrate at the North Carolina Pickle Festival in early April. Or you can turn out with the local residents for the annual New Year's Eve Pickle Drop, held at the civilized hour of seven in the evening (which is midnight Greenwich Mean Time) at the corner of Cucumber and Vine. Where else?

MT. OLIVE PICKLE COMPANY, INC.

Corner of Cucumber and Vine

One Cucumber Boulevard

P.O. Box 609

Mount Olive, N.C. 28365

800-672-5041

www.mtolivepickles.com

CELEBRATING THE PUNGENT RAMP

RAMPS, OR WILD LEEKS, have been known for centuries as nature's first spring delicacy. The mountain people of the Southeast particularly prize the vegetables. The flavor and odor are usually compared to a combination of onions and garlic. Ramps frequently grow in patches of hundreds or thousands in the rich soil of maple-beech-hemlock hardwoods.

Early mountain settlers had a special appreciation for ramps after a winter of dried and cured foods. In the 1930s, area residents routinely searched for ramps in the early spring not only for flavoring dishes but also for use in making spring tonics. That's when word of the practice began to spread to the curious, entertainment-seeking folk of the Piedmont and flatlands.

Bear in mind that ramps are so pungent that even those who love them best will tell you to keep your distance for several days after you've eaten a mess of them. Mountain children have sometimes been sent home from school because of excessive ramp odor. Food writer Jane Snow described the flavor profile of ramps as resembling "fried green onions with a dash of funky feet." Mmm-mmm.

Because they have such an overwhelming taste, ramps are most often used in other dishes—fried with potatoes, eggs, or pinto beans, for example. Given the strong current interest in heritage foods, it isn't surprising that ramps have recently become trendy in white-tablecloth restaurants.

The North Carolina Ramp Festival takes place in early May each year in Waynesville.

At the North Carolina Ramp Festival, contestants try to consume the most raw ramp bulbs.
LINDA DICKINSON

It's recognized as the oldest such festival in the world. Similar events are held up and down the Appalachian chain from western Maryland to Georgia, and the different dates of the celebrations allow enthusiasts to go ramp festival hopping. The timing of a festival depends on a town's elevation and latitude, since those factors determine when the snow melts and therefore when ramps grow.

Except for those cultivated on one ramp farm in West Virginia, the odiferous plants grow in the wild. Because thousands of tourists show up for many ramp festivals, there is some concern that intensive harvesting may threaten the abundance of the wild leeks. The Appalachian ramp festivals collectively spur the gathering and consumption of some thirty-two hundred pounds of ramps in an average year. Harvests have been banned

since 2002 in Great Smoky Mountains National Park in North Carolina and Tennessee, so more people are collecting them in nearby national forests. Research is under way into how to best manage the supply of ramps for future generations, including the development of practices for the cultivation of the vegetable.

That might become necessary in the future, but somehow it just won't be the same.

NORTH CAROLINA RAMP FESTIVAL

American Legion North Carolina Post 47
171 Legion Drive
Waynesville, N.C. 28786
828-456-8691

Livermush

THE POOR MAN'S PÂTÉ

Jan Karon, a native of the foothills town of Lenoir, North Carolina, and the author of the Mitford/Father Tim series of novels, had a moment of inspiration in creating the character of Russell Jacks, a small-town church sexton with an abiding craving for livermush, the food with perhaps the most terrible-sounding name on the face of the earth. Here's a man who earns his keep caring for the grounds of a church known as Lord's Chapel who's nourished by an exceptionally earthbound taste, the livermush delivered to him on a regular basis by his pastor. Readers are hooked immediately.

This regional concoction, despite having both *liver* and *mush* in its name, not only endures but actually thrives in a crescent stretching from Greensboro to the foothills west of Charlotte. Outside this "livermush band," you may be able to buy the product or one of its close cousins in the grocery store, but you probably cannot order it in a restaurant. That's no big loss to those who say,

"Livermush? Whatever that is, it sounds really gross."

Actually, it doesn't look all that great either.

In a stretch of lovely countryside outside Shelby, two small food-processing plants sit within a mile of one another. Considering how dearly the residents of Cleveland County love livermush, a homely mixture of pig parts and cornmeal, it's ironic, yet appropriate, that Jenkins Foods and Mack's Livermush and Meats chose to build their facilities overlooking scenic fields of grain rolling toward the distant mountains. If the taste of livermush is a foreshadowing of heaven, as most locals believe, shouldn't the place where it's made have a heavenly exterior aspect as well?

But then it's worth considering the contrast between the beauty of the foothills surrounding these humble facilities and the off-putting appearance of vats of steaming brown glop inside the plants, soon to become cold, one-pound blocks of livermush. It's an apt reminder that

Livermush is very similar to scrapple, although some scrapple may not contain pork liver; livermush always does. Both contain minced pork, seasonings, and cornmeal.
UNC-TV

while heaven may be on the way, we're yet bound to this earthly vale of woe.

All that being said, I'm one former skeptic who now believes livermush is a pretty heavenly food.

So what is it? A down-to-earth combination of meat from the hog's head and other pork scraps, cornmeal, and pork liver (at least 30 percent liver by law). Meat and bones are simmered to make a stock, after which the deboned meat is finely ground and added back into the liquid. Cornmeal, sage, salt, black pepper, and red pepper are stirred into the bubbling, gurgling mixture. When it has thickened sufficiently, it's poured into large pans and cooled. The solidified livermush is cut and packaged in bricks, from which it is

ordinarily cut into slices and fried.

To get an idea of the flavor profile, imagine finely ground mild pork sausage with a cornmeal taste and a hint of liver, similar to what you might find in braunschweiger (liverwurst). Pork liver does not have nearly as strong a taste or as distinctive a texture as beef or chicken liver. Many people who don't "do" other types of liver get along just fine with livermush, particularly because of its appealing crunch when fried.

Because livermush is one of those foods that grew out of times of scarcity, when food supplies had to be stretched and nearly everything was used up, you might imagine that it's a disappearing local oddity, enjoyed mostly by senior citizens. But nothing could be farther from the truth. Livermush seems consistently popular and highly regarded across all age groups in North Carolina's central and southwest Piedmont. You'll often see small children enjoying crispy slices of fried livermush in restaurants located roughly between Interstates 85 and 40. Surprisingly, it isn't really a "guy" thing either. Most versions of the pork loaf contain parts such as pig spleens and snouts ("snoots" to the locals). Nonetheless, an impressive number of females in the livermush crescent are devotees of this "poor man's pâté."

The unlovely dish provides shock value, which is part of the fun of belonging to the livermush culture. Livermush enthusiasts, male and female, sometimes can't resist triggering the "eww" response. A recent YouTube video showed a group of high-school girls from somewhere west of the Yadkin River explaining their fondness for livermush. They took great delight in asserting that the dish contains pig ears, appendixes, tails, and intestines, which is untrue, if entertaining. In another YouTube video, a faux-sounding foothills redneck presenting himself as "Clem Hunsucker" maintains with a straight face that livermush also contains pork brains and pig feet. While that may be true of some homemade versions, no commercial livermush includes those items. But why ruin a good rural legend?

Livermush pride is perhaps nowhere more prominently on display than in Cleveland County, which calls itself "the Livermush Capital of the World." One of the main reasons for that appears to be that during the early 1930s, when commercial livermush pro-

duction was getting started, Cleveland County largely escaped the effects of a swine disease affecting many other areas of the South. The ailment rendered pig livers from many locales unfit for consumption. Since pigs from Cleveland County were spared, the county grew into something of a center for livermush production. Over the years, one of the most visible duties of the various mayors of Shelby, the Cleveland County seat, has been to serve as an unofficial but enthusiastic spokesman for livermush.

Livermush is quite similar to—some would say indistinguishable from—scrapple, which came to this country with the Pennsylvania Dutch and is still largely a regional specialty of eastern Pennsylvania, Maryland, Delaware, and the vicinity of Washington, D.C. Scrapple, originally known as *panhas* (spelled several different ways), first contained buckwheat to help thicken a stock of pork scraps and spices. Over time, the buckwheat was replaced by cornmeal in most versions.

German settlers are thought to have taken the recipe for scrapple with them as they left Pennsylvania in search of available land for settlement, moving down the Great Wagon Road through Virginia's Shenandoah Valley and into the North Carolina Piedmont during the second half of the eighteenth century. A little over a century and a half later, the North Carolina version of the dish had become known as livermush, and most of its fans had begun to think of it as something unique to the state's central and southwest Piedmont.

There are still Pennsylvania foodies who

claim, tongue in cheek, that livermush is exactly the same as scrapple and that we have basically stolen one of their state's signature dishes and slapped a new name on it. But this seems to be a spurious claim, in that while scrapple can and sometimes does contain pork liver, other versions don't have any liver at all, whereas North Carolina law stipulates that livermush must be made of at least one-third liver.

In *The Mitford Bedside Companion*, Jan Karon writes, "True livermush is as rare as hen's teeth and is found only in North Carolina. Indeed, once it travels over the state line, it becomes Scrapple, which is to livermush what the carpetbag was to the South."

Liver pudding is a widely available cousin to livermush. According to local lore, this product is basically livermush sold anywhere east of the Yadkin River. It can be found in most grocery stores across the state, even in eastern North Carolina, whereas the product labeled *livermush* is nearly always found in the Piedmont and foothills. Neese's, the Greensboro producer of country sausage and many other pork products, used to package and label the exact same product as *liver pudding* in most areas and *livermush* west of the Yadkin. Nowadays, Neese's recipes for liver pudding and livermush are slightly different. The pudding is supposed to be a slightly smoother "cold cut," while the mush is described as being "slightly drier." But to be honest, I would probably fail a blind taste test in identifying the respective versions. Neese's has also started producing a product it calls Country Scrapple, which contains liver. In point of

fact, it tastes remarkably similar to the other two. All of them contain cornmeal, all fry up with a crispy crust, and all are delicious, in my estimation.

Some livermush producers describe their product as a low-fat food, but you should know that livermush was selected by Health.com as North Carolina's entry in an online article entitled "50 Fattiest Foods in the States," earning its place alongside such delectables as Alabama's bacon-wrapped meat loaf, Indiana's fried pork brain sandwich, and Wisconsin's deep-fried cheese curds. Actually, though, livermush falls into the "average" category for both fat and calories. A three-ounce portion of most brands has six grams of fat, half of it saturated, which is nowhere near the fancifully estimated fat content of the home recipe on which the Health.com assessment was based—an unbelievable thirty grams per serving. Livermush is rather high in cholesterol, however, so it should be consumed in moderation.

During the extreme food scarcities of the Civil War and Reconstruction, livermush was prized as one way of helping anyone fortunate enough to have a hog to use every available scrap of meat. The survival habits of those years took root, and livermush's reputation as an economical dish ensured its being prepared in many homes through the turn of the century and the early decades of the 1900s. But what some lightheartedly refer to as "the modern livermush era" began in the 1920s, when families began to make livermush for sale, rather than strictly for home consumption.

Bert and Carrie Mae Canipe, who lived

near Shelby, began one of the area's first livermush businesses in 1926. Mack's Livermush got started in 1933, when founder Ray McKee began production. During the early years, a one-pound brick of livermush could be purchased for ten cents. Older Cleveland County residents were fond of saying, "We could never have made it through the Depression without livermush." Even today, at about $2.50 per pound, the product is a valuable recession-fighting tool for struggling families. Ron McKee, grandson of the founder, who now runs Mack's Livermush, says his company produces about eighty thousand pounds per month.

During the 1930s, livermush was made in ten-pound pans, and the pans themselves were taken to the store and placed in the meat case, sometimes while still warm. Livermush wasn't packaged and sold in one-pound blocks until the early 1940s. Nowadays, hand-held wooden stirring paddles have been replaced by electric agitators, and stainless-steel steam kettles have taken the place of cast-iron kettles set over wood fires. The distribution network for Mack's Livermush has expanded dramatically from the early years but is still limited to towns and cities within a two-and-a-half-hour radius of Cleveland County, including Charlotte, Asheville, Hickory, Lenoir, and Greenville, South Carolina.

Jenkins Foods and Mack's in Cleveland County, Corriher's in Rowan County, Hunter's in McDowell County, and Neese's in Guilford County are North Carolina's chief livermush producers, although there are several smaller, local producers such as Fitzhugh

McMurry, who sells his product only out of the meat case at McMurry's Store and Farms in Cleveland County. His livermush comes from a family recipe that isn't really a recipe, in that nothing is measured and no two batches are exactly the same. While many versions use fatty scraps from pig heads, McMurry's livermush features leaner cuts from pork shoulders and backbone, often from home-raised pigs.

In his book *The Whole Beast*, British chef Fergus Henderson writes, "If you're going to kill the animal, it seems only polite to use the whole thing." This attitude seems to reflect a trend in recent years toward a nose-to-tail mindset among chefs. That has helped boost the popularity of livermush, along with similar meat products. Henderson's work highlights the flavor and usefulness of tripe, trotters, and internal organs of the pig. The concept seems to be spreading. Jon Fasman, a food communist, recently observed in *More Intelligent Life* magazine, "Since nobody really wants to come to dinner and find a plate of hearts and snouts steaming on the table, scrapple (or in this case livermush) . . . turns those unwieldy bits into positively G-rated form."

All that may be true, but the average person probably would be wise not to witness the process through which pig parts are crafted into livermush. In an unlikely move, the Travel Channel's *Taste of America* program once visited Shelby to produce a segment on the manufacture of livermush. Despite the old saying about the inadvisability of watching either laws or sausage being made, the producers of the program focused almost entirely on the process of cooking, mixing, forming, and packaging livermush, rather than the history of and love for the dish. Not only that, the host raised the ire of local residents by repeatedly referring on camera to "livermoosh." Let's face it, if there's one thing that sounds worse than livermush, it's livermoosh. What were they thinking?

Far better to evoke images of a perfectly browned slice of livermush cozying up to a couple of sunny-side-up eggs and a plump biscuit. Its crisp cornmeal exterior, contrasting beautifully with a soft, savory interior, provides a wonderful accompaniment to eggs and grits. You can break up livermush into bits and scramble it with eggs, or you can go even farther than that. For example, the so-called Mayor's Special at the Shelby Café features livermush scrambled with eggs and cheese and folded into a pita sandwich, most often with a slathering of mayonnaise. Shelby Café co-owner George Ritzkallah has also developed a popular breakfast casserole that contains livermush, eggs, mushroom soup, cheese, and onions.

Fried livermush is also a versatile sandwich meat, nestled on a hamburger bun and topped with slaw or lettuce, tomato, and

Livermush fans like it on a sandwich for lunch, as a breakfast meat, or even as an omelet filling.
UNC-TV

mayonnaise. It also sits with aplomb between slices of white or wheat toast, perhaps topped with a fried egg. Ron McKee of Mack's Livermush says one of his favorite snacks is a slice of fried livermush on a bun or a piece of toast, generously spread with jelly or preserves. At least one pizza restaurant in nearby Boiling Springs, home of Gardner-Webb University, has experimented with using crispy bits of fried livermush as a pizza topping, in place of sausage.

Personally, I love livermush best as an alternative to pâté—warmed in the microwave for a few seconds, spread on toast points, maybe sprinkled with a little chopped sweet onion, and anointed with a smear of Dijon mustard or Texas Pete Honey Mustard Sauce. Some livermush producers offer hot and spicy versions for the adventurous.

You can sample a wide variety of livermush presentations at the Shelby Fall Festival and Livermush Expo, which takes place every October, or at the annual Livermush Festival, held each June in the McDowell County town of Marion, the production site for Hunter's Livermush.

Tamra Wilson, in an essay for Charlotte's WFAE public radio, noted that "the North Carolina Piedmont is where scrapple-wise German settlers called it quits after lumbering down the Great Wagon road in the eighteenth century. We can thank them for turning this into the Land of Livermush. We can credit the lean years of history for keeping it that way."

Amen.

BOB GARNER'S LIVERMUSH SHEPHERD'S PIE

1½ pounds livermush
2 medium onions, diced
1 tablespoon sugar
10½-ounce can cream of mushroom
   soup
6 medium potatoes
½ stick butter
½ to 1 cup milk
salt and pepper to taste
2 cups grated cheese

Cut livermush into ½-inch slices and fry until crispy. Drain slices on paper towels, then lay them edge to edge to cover bottom of a 9-by-13-inch baking dish. Sauté onions until well browned; sprinkle sugar over onions as they're frying to help them caramelize. Spread sautéed onions over livermush slices. Using a rubber spatula, spread undiluted soup over onions and livermush. Peel and boil potatoes to make mashed potatoes; add butter and milk before whipping. Add salt and pepper and spread potatoes in an even layer on top of mushroom soup, onions, and livermush. Top casserole with grated cheese and bake at 400 degrees for about 30 minutes until cheese is bubbly and beginning to brown. Serve on plates with ketchup or your favorite steak sauce.

FEATURE ATTRACTIONS

SHELBY CAFÉ

This cheerful "on the square" eatery has been around for nearly a century and still gets high marks not only for the food but for the sense of permanence it engenders. "OK, four stars might be pushing it," wrote one fan in an online review, "but it gets an extra for the nostalgia factor."

Shelby Café may be the classic meat-and-three eatery, but like many memorable small-town restaurants, it has at various times been owned and managed by restaurateurs of Greek heritage. Greek café owners tend to nail Southern cooking—or indeed any cuisine intended primarily for common folk—but they can also add a touch or two of Mediterranean magic. A case in point is Shelby Café's house salad dressing, which is described as "oily, red, tangy and top secret." Customers have remarked that they would drink it through a straw if they thought no one was watching.

Breakfast is served all day at the café, and livermush—deep-fried or browned on a flat-top grill—is a featured breakfast meat, together with bacon, sausage, and fried bologna (another tradition passed down by the many German settlers in the North Carolina Piedmont). The cooks will prepare your livermush pretty much to order, and they'll serve it inside a fluffy biscuit, next to fried eggs and grits, worked into a livermush and cheese omelet, or muddled into a breakfast casserole with eggs, cheese, mushroom soup, and sautéed onions.

For lunch, the aforementioned Mayor's Special livermush-in-a-pita sandwich is a favorite, with eggs, cheese, and mayonnaise pillowing the main ingredient.

The café's regularly changing menu features daily specials including fried chicken and meat loaf and favorite sides such as squash casserole, buttermilk cornbread, and fried okra. The locals all say the desserts are a high point as well, although I've never had room to get that far.

SHELBY CAFÉ

220 South Lafayette Street

Shelby, N.C. 28150

704-487-8461

Breakfast and lunch daily; dinner, Monday through Friday

WINDY CITY GRILL

Three things have characterized Hickory's Windy City Grill during its sixty or so years of existence. The first is that it serves only sandwiches and hot dogs, so the terrific breakfasts here all come between two pieces of some kind of bread. The second is that since Hickory is a blue-collar place, and the grill is a working-class joint, many people show up in work attire. The third is that a lot of Hickory residents are of German ancestry, so the grill serves plenty of livermush and fried bologna. Students from nearby Lenoir-Rhyne College

The Shelby Café, where livermush is always on the menu, is a longstanding, on-the-square restaurant in downtown Shelby.
MIKE ONIFFREY

frequent the place as well, primarily because the prices are reasonable and they don't have to dress up.

The menu features some pretty elaborate breakfast sandwiches—livermush, bologna, ham, bacon, sausage, cheese, and eggs—artfully loaded onto a roll or piled on toast. One of the most famous breakfast standbys is the

sausage and egg sandwich with double cheese, served on a bun. Crispy, deep-fried livermush forms the base layer of several other breakfast favorites, with cheese, eggs, and jelly being the most-ordered coverings.

For lunch, customers can try a livermush sandwich on a bun with either lettuce, tomato, and mayonnaise or slaw and mustard. The

Livermush | 125

fried bologna goes well with slaw and the special house chili. And Windy City's famous hot dogs, when ordered as "regular," come topped with mustard, chili, onions, and slaw.

This restaurant has occupied at least three different locations over the years. It was once known as Homer's; a giant-sized burger named for the former owner is still on the menu.

Windy City Grill is especially packed on Saturdays, but the drive-through moves along at a good clip. If you don't mind jostling for a seat inside, this high-energy café is one of the main places in town to see, and be seen by, all your friends.

WINDY CITY GRILL

2514 North Center Street

Hickory, N.C. 28601

828-322-1131

Breakfast and lunch, Monday through Saturday

This event, held each year in October around Shelby's historic Court Square, was formerly called the Shelby Fall Livermush Festival. Activities vary from year to year, but visitors can count on arts and crafts, children's activities, music, and, of course, opportunities to sample livermush prepared in ways traditional and inventive. Most participating restaurant offer at least one special livermush dish.

OFFICIAL NORTH CAROLINA FALL LIVERMUSH FESTIVAL

Uptown Shelby Association

211 South Trade Street

Shelby, N.C. 28150

704-484-3100

The counter at Hickory's Windy City Grill is nearly always busy, due at least in part to its livermush sandwiches.
UNC-TV

MARION LIVERMUSH FESTIVAL

Marion is the home of Hunter's Livermush, which usually offers free sandwiches during this annual event, slated for June. This is an evening festival, scheduled from six-thirty to nine o'clock in downtown Marion. The winner of the Best Dressed Pig Contest (which could be a child, an adult, a Harley-Davidson motorcycle, or even an actual pig) wins twenty-five dollars. Live music serves as a background for the livermush-sandwich-eating contest and the cornhole tournament.

MCDOWELL COUNTY TOURISM DEVELOPMENT AUTHORITY

25 U.S. 70 West
Old Fort, N.C. 28762
888-233-6111 or 828-652-2215
www.mcdowellnc.org

BRIGHT LEAF HOT DOGS

AT HILLBILLIES in Zebulon, April Hagwood asks customers ordering a hot dog, "Brown or red?"

"Brown" refers to an all-beef hot dog. "Red" means a Bright Leaf brand hot dog, made by Smithfield's Carolina Packers. Hagwood tells customers it's a pork dog, to differentiate it from the alternative, but it's actually made with both pork and beef. It contains no chicken, unlike some other red hot dogs.

"Red outsells brown by ten to one," says Hagwood. "But you know, a Yankee who comes in here will not order a red dog."

That does not seem to be the case everywhere. Bruce Kraig, a Chicago college professor, is the author of *Hot Dog: A Global History*. As part of his research, he conducted a taste test with 150 people in New York City and found that they preferred Bright Leaf red hot dogs over Oscar Meyer.

Kraig says all hot dogs were red in former days. During the 1960s, concerns emerged that a commonly used red food dye might cause cancer, so many hot dog manufacturers stopped using red dyes. In the South, though, some simply switched to other red dyes—those used to color cough syrup and cherry soda—so they could keep the traditional color.

"We started with the red. We continued with the red," says Jean Jones, president and CEO of Carolina Packers, the last remaining major hot dog maker in North Carolina. Her late husband, Buck, inherited Carolina Packers from his father, founder John Jones Sr. The company has been making hot dogs—along with smoked sausage, bologna, and chili—since 1941.

The Bright Leaf name refers to the section of U.S. 301 in Smithfield where Carolina Packers is located, which has long been known as Brightleaf Boulevard. That's because of the number of tobacco warehouses that lined the highway during the 1940s. The tobacco leaf logo on packages of the red hot

Bright Leaf hot dogs love all toppings, especially chili, mustard, slaw, and onions.

dogs is a clear reminder of eastern Carolina's agricultural heritage.

Bright Leaf hot dogs don't have the shelf life of other brands. Somehow, that seems to have become a plus, rather than a drawback, as many customers apparently consider them fresher. The hot dogs last only fifteen to twenty days after they leave the plant in Smithfield, as opposed to the hundred days touted for competing brands. They don't contain the number of preservatives found in other hot dogs and aren't vacuum-packed. Being a small company, Carolina Packers produces its hot dogs in small batches, which allows it to monitor sales more closely.

Carolina Packers general manager Kent Denning, who worked at the plant in high school, says several days of rain noticeably slow sales because people don't get outside to grill hot dogs. When area schools are out, sales go up because students need a quick lunch at home.

At grills and lunch counters, the red Bright Leaf hot dogs are most often served on steamed buns with chili, mustard, and slaw, although many diners go one step farther and order them "all the way," with onions added.

Bright Leaf hot dogs are usually available at Piggly Wiggly, Walmart, IGA, Food Lion, Kroger, and Lowe's Foods stores in eastern North Carolina. Carolina Packers delivers to a few grocery stores and restaurants in the central Piedmont, but not much farther west than that. (One of the most famous Piedmont outposts for Carolina Packers is Yum Yum, a hot dog and ice-cream shop adjacent to the campus of UNC-Greensboro that's always a top vote-getter in best-hot-dog-in-North-Carolina conversations.) At the plant, however, employees regularly pack personal orders and ship them all across the country, mostly to North Carolina expatriates. They'll ship whatever people want—including bologna, smoked sausage, and chili—but the overwhelming majority of requests are for hot dogs.

BRIGHT LEAF HOT DOGS

Carolina Packers

2999 South Brightleaf Boulevard

Smithfield, N.C. 27577

919-934-2181

www.carolinapackers.com

Moravian Cooking
SPICE COOKIES, SUGAR CAKE, AND CHICKEN PIE

The culinary heritage of Winston-Salem and the surrounding area has been influenced by many cultures. But it has a particular, unique connection to Eastern Europe because of the city's having grown out of Moravian settlements.

The Moravian denomination originated in what was once Czechoslovakia. Under the influence of John Hus of Bohemia, it predated Martin Luther by a century in breaking away from the Roman Catholic Church. Remnants of the original Moravian adherents, who had been heavily persecuted, settled and reestablished their church in Germany. Their descendants came to America in the eighteenth century, settling first in Bethlehem, Pennsylvania, then in North Carolina.

In 1753, a tiny band of Moravians began settling a large tract called Wachovia, which included the site of what is now Winston-Salem. After establishing their original settlements of Bethabara and Bethania, they founded their central community of Salem, meaning "peace," in 1766. From the beginning, Salem was known for its craftsmen, who produced tools, ceramics, furniture, metal goods, and, most importantly to readers of this book, food!

In 1849, the church sold land adjacent to Salem for a new town, which was subsequently named Winston in honor of Major Joseph Winston, a local hero of the Revolutionary War. Winston eventually grew to be three times larger than Salem, and the two towns merged in 1913.

Salem began to suffer from neglect. Old Salem, Inc., was formed in 1950 with the goal of saving around ten historically significant buildings. Meticulous recordkeeping by the Moravian Church, including details about buildings and landscapes, was a huge help in the preservation effort. Today, the Old Salem Historic District includes eighty-seven acres. Old Salem, maintained as a living-history museum and national historic site, offers a re-creation of Salem as it existed between the years 1766 and 1840. At many of the twenty buildings and gardens included with a paid admission, costumed guides demonstrate metalworking, shoemaking, and pottery making. Several shops are open to the public without an admission ticket. One of these is Winkler Bakery, which bakes traditional treats such as Moravian sugar cake and wafer-thin Moravian cookies on-site.

Along with the many-pointed Moravian star, sweet and savory baked creations probably symbolize more than anything else the Winston-Salem area and its unusual history. Moravian cookies, sugar cake, and chicken pie are the culinary landmarks of Winston-Salem and much of the northern Piedmont.

Moravian cooks may be known above all else for their signature spice (or ginger) cook-

Sugar and ginger are the top-selling Moravian cookies, although many other varieties are available.

Foods That Make You Say Mmm-mmm

ies, descendants of the German *lebkuchen*. A cultural grafting occurred after many religious faithful fled Moravia in what is now the Czech Republic and settled in Germany for a period of time. True to the German custom, the Moravians referred to the cookies as "cakes" in their earliest written notations. They were traditionally baked for family and friends during the Christmas holidays.

The Moravian cookies that most of us have purchased in cardboard tubes contain an exotic, non-subtle spice blend. Most of the historic ginger cookie recipes call for dense, dark molasses, ginger, aromatic cloves, and cinnamon. Why these particular ingredients? For one thing, they are all hearty spices with a long shelf life, which was important in a frontier settlement.

Thanks to some unique baking techniques, the cookies are incredibly thin and crispy—so much so that some refer to them as "glass cookies," since they readily shatter if dropped. But were the sheets of dough not rolled out to an incredibly thin state, the cookies would probably have a dense, impossible-to-chew texture. The thinly rolled dough not only provides a satisfyingly crisp texture but also has the advantage of baking relatively quickly. Fewer minutes per batch means more batches can be baked in an allotted time!

Traditional recipes calling for hefty quantities of ingredients produced many batches of cookies. It was common to store cookie dough for days or weeks during the winter months. As the dough rested, the flavors intensified.

Spice is the best known of the Moravian cookies. But today, customers can also choose from among sugar, orange and cranberry spice, lemon, chocolate, black walnut, and Key lime, to name just some of the flavors available.

Moravian sugar cake is a yeast-raised, sweetened bread topped with a thick, rich mixture of butter, sugar, and cinnamon. Some scholars say it was originally baked in large, round loaves that were broken apart and served during Moravian Lovefeasts, which are congregational services dedicated to strengthening bonds of brotherly love. For a long, long time, though, sugar cake has been baked in large, rectangular jellyroll pans. It resembles focaccia bread, with a creviced surface in which the butter and sugar topping collect.

Over the last two-hundred-plus years, sugar cake has been consumed regularly on Shrove Tuesday (the day before Ash Wednesday, which marks the beginning of Lent). It is also traditionally served on Easter morning and is enormously popular at Christmas as well.

As is common in Eastern European recipes, most traditional versions of Moravian sugar cake contain mashed potatoes, as well as the water used to cook the potatoes.

Moravian chicken pie is a rich, solid, meat-only pie that is different from chicken pot pie, which contains vegetables. It is most often associated with the eighteenth-century Moravian settlers but also seems to be traditional among cooks of German ancestry whose forebears were not members of the Moravian movement. It may, in fact, have been adopted from the Germans after remnants of Europe's original Protestant denomination left Bohemia and Czechoslovakia and regrouped in Germany under the patronage of Nicholas von Zinzendorf. So in addition to being a Moravian standby, the pie is also a favorite potluck dish among the Baptists and Methodists of the North Carolina Piedmont. The old version uses the entire chicken, both dark and white meat, while newer recipes seem to gravitate toward white meat only. Nearly every recipe also includes a rich chicken gravy, which is served over the pie's top crust. It's a simple, classic comfort food, hearty and eminently satisfying.

Many Piedmont families serve Moravian chicken pie with green beans and corn, which may be considered something of an unusual combination in other regions. The pie is beautifully complemented, especially during autumn, by another old, traditional dish from the region: persimmon pudding.

Following are recipes for the three Moravian favorites.

MORAVIAN SPICE COOKIES

1 quart molasses

¾ pound brown sugar

2 tablespoons ground cloves

2 tablespoons ground ginger

2 tablespoons ground cinnamon

¾ pound shortening

2 tablespoons baking soda

3¼ pounds flour

This recipe makes a lot of cookies. You may choose to halve or even quarter it.

In a heavy-bottomed saucepan, heat molasses, brown sugar, spices, and shortening over medium heat until shortening is melted and mixture is uniform. Do not let it scorch! Add baking soda and mix well until it is dissolved. The mixture will be very foamy. Remove from heat, pour into a large, heat-proof mixing bowl, and let cool to room temperature. When cool, add flour. Mix until flour is fully incorporated, roll into a ball, wrap

tightly in plastic wrap, and refrigerate overnight.

The next day, remove dough from refrigerator, preheat oven to 325 degrees, and prepare a large cutting board or countertop by sprinkling liberally with flour; flour your rolling pin, too. Line a cookie sheet with parchment paper. Cut off a fist-sized chunk of dough and return the rest to the refrigerator while you work. At this point, it is important to work quickly while the dough is still cool. Roll dough until it is uniformly ¼ to ⅛ inch thick; don't be afraid to use more flour to prevent dough from sticking to the board or the rolling pin. Cut out cookies using whatever shape cookie cutter you wish, gently brush off any excess flour with a pastry brush, and place on parchment-lined cookie sheet; a thin spatula will help to move the cookies. Bake for 7 to 10 minutes until barely browned around the edges.

Repeat the process with the remaining dough, remembering to work quickly and to keep the dough chilled. The dough keeps quite well in the freezer, so you can roll out the sheets and freeze them for up to 3 months for future use. Just remove from freezer and let rest at room temperature for 5 to 10 minutes before cutting, then bake as directed above.

HELENA COUCH'S MORAVIAN SUGAR CAKE

CAKE

1 cup hot mashed potatoes

1 cup sugar

1 package dry yeast, dissolved in 1 cup warm water

¾ cup margarine, melted and cooled

2 eggs, beaten

1 teaspoon salt

4 cups flour

TOPPING

1 stick cold butter

1 pound light brown sugar

cinnamon

Mix first 6 cake ingredients in order given. Sift in flour 1 cup at a time, mixing thoroughly after each cup. Let rise for 6 to 8 hours or overnight until at least double in bulk. Stir down.

Spread cake batter in four 8-inch pans or two 9-by-13-inch pans greased only on the bottom. Let rise 2 hours or until light and puffy.

Cut butter into ¼-inch pats. Push pats into batter about 1 inch apart. Spread light brown sugar over batter and dust with cinnamon.

Bake at 350 degrees for 20 to 30 minutes until brown. Sugar cake is good warm and also freezes well. Recipe may be doubled or tripled.

This recipe comes courtesy of Margaret Couch.

MORAVIAN CHICKEN PIE

PASTRY

2 cups sifted all-purpose flour

1 teaspoon salt

¾ cup Crisco

6 to 8 tablespoons cold water

FILLING

3 cups cooked chopped chicken, both light and dark meat

¼ cup flour

1¼ cups homemade chicken broth (or ¾ cup canned chicken broth diluted with ½ cup water)

salt and pepper to taste

Combine flour and salt. Cut in Crisco. Add cold water and mix into soft dough, handling as little as possible. Roll out half the dough to fit a greased 10-inch pie plate.

Fill pie with chicken. Dust with flour. Pour chicken broth to cover. Add salt and pepper.

Roll out second half of dough for top crust. Pinch edges of crust together to seal. Flute around the edges. Bake at 375 to 400 degrees for 45 to 60 minutes.

This recipe is from *Fries Memorial Moravian Church: History, Customs, Recipes.*

FEATURE ATTRACTIONS

MRS. HANES' MORAVIAN COOKIES

Before you embark on the earlier recipe for Moravian spice cookies, you may want to consider touring Mrs. Hanes' Moravian Cookies in Clemmons to absorb some pointers on rolling out the dough to the ideal thinness and on cutting the cookies. Mrs. Hanes' cookie-making team hand-rolls and hand-cuts more than 115,000 pounds of dough per year, which represents over ten million cookies—each one cut with a cookie cutter!

Following your tour, you may decide to let Mrs. Hanes and her staff do your cookie baking for you.

MRS. HANES' MORAVIAN COOKIES

4643 Friedburg Church Road
Clemmons, N.C. 27102
336-764-1402
www.hanescookies.com
Open Monday through Saturday; open daily for expanded hours during the holiday season. Call or consult the website for schedule.

TAVERN IN OLD SALEM

The Tavern in Old Salem has expanded and tweaked its menu significantly during recent years, but Moravian chicken pie is a long-time classic choice here. One can purchase a whole baked pie as well. Lori Keiper, one of the owners of the tavern, is also a pastry chef, so the pies draw rave reviews for their crusts.

TAVERN IN OLD SALEM

736 South Main Street
Winston-Salem, N.C. 27101
336-722-1227
thetaverninoldsalem.ws
Lunch, Tuesday through Sunday; dinner, Tuesday through Saturday. Call for holiday schedule.

The Tavern in Old Salem serves a Moravian chicken pie entrée, or you can purchase an entire pie to take home.
THE TAVERN IN OLD SALEM

DEWEY'S AND SALEM BAKING COMPANY

DEWEY'S BAKERY has made some huge organizational changes in recent years, but none of them has diminished in the slightest the company's image as a small, local bakery lovingly founded on heritage. Nor should they.

It helps that the place is identified by a first name, as in "Joe's Grocery" or "Frank's Place." The Dewey who made the place famous was Dewey G. Wilkerson, who opened the bakery in downtown Winston-Salem in 1930. From the beginning, the bakery fed on (and literally fed) the Moravian cooking traditions that form part of the bedrock of Winston-Salem's history: Moravian sugar cake, Moravian cookies, and Moravian Lovefeast buns. Oh, the bakery does a wonderful job with cupcakes, coffee cakes (the "Grandpa" and "Grandma" varieties are favorites), bar cookies and squares, cheese straws, biscuits, scones—you name it—but Moravian specialties are the very air breathed at Dewey's.

This was the first all-electric bakery in the area, operating in several downtown Winston-Salem locations over the years. During World War II, when sugar was rationed, housewives ordering cakes from Dewey's helped pay for them by substituting a cup of sugar for part of the cash price. In 1955, the bakery was destroyed by fire on Easter Monday. But thanks to heavy support from the city's citizens, Dewey's moved to its current main location in the Thruway Shopping Center. (It also operates other permanent locations around town, in addition to dozens of holiday-season "pop-up" stores.)

Dewey's bakes more than five hundred different made-from-scratch items as part of its normal year-round business. Employment routinely doubles during the holiday rush. Moravian sugar cake, in particular, is baked pretty much twenty-four hours per day from October through December.

In 1992, Salem Baking Company was created alongside Dewey's to focus on the same traditional products for distribution around the world, and also for adding other products such as cheese straws, cheese biscuits, and shortbread. For several years, the division has sold its baked goods as a wholesale brand throughout the country to retailers including Williams-Sonoma and Fresh Market, to independent gift shops, and to specialty stores.

Scott Livengood, a former Krispy Kreme CEO, purchased a 50 percent share of the company in 2006. He and his wife have had full ownership of Dewey's since 2012. The change has resulted in the opening of new kinds of stores. Having previously opened Dewey's Wedding Cake Boutique, a by-appointment business in downtown Winston-Salem, the company also ventured into a new concept store called Cake by Dewey's in Hanes Mall. Additionally, Dewey's acquired Blue Ridge Ice Creams for its Thruway Shopping Center location, thus providing the perfect marriage of cake and ice cream under one roof.

DEWEY'S BAKERY

262 South Stratford Road
Winston-Salem, N.C. 27103
336-725-8321
www.deweysbakery.com

SALEM BAKING COMPANY

224 South Cherry Street
Winston-Salem, N.C. 27101
336-748-0230
www.salembaking.com

Moravian sugar cake, cookies, and cheese straws are just some of the delicacies found at Dewey's Bakery.
DEWEY'S BAKERY

KRISPY KREME: HOT DOUGHNUTS NOW

MANY NORTH CAROLINIANS have heard the story about how Krispy Kreme founder Vernon Rudolph bought his secret yeast-raised doughnut recipe from a French chef in New Orleans, then rented a building in Winston-Salem and, in 1937, began selling doughnuts to local grocery stores.

Not too many people know, though, that Rudolph actually acquired his recipe four years earlier, in 1933, and that before opening in Winston-Salem, he and an uncle first bought Joseph LeBeouf's doughnut shop in Paducah, Kentucky. Substituting his recipe for LeBeouf's, Rudolph began selling out of his shop and also delivering doughnuts on his bicycle. The operation moved from Paducah to Nashville, Tennessee, where other members of Rudolph's family joined the venture. Finally, Rudolph sold his interest in the Nashville store in 1937—and that's when he set up shop in Winston-Salem.

As the delicious aroma of cooking doughnuts wafted into the streets of what later became Old Salem, passersby began stopping to ask if they could buy hot doughnuts. Before long, Rudolph cut a hole in an outside wall and began selling directly to walk-up customers.

Ever since, Krispy Kreme has continued to wrestle with its identity. It is part packaged-goods company selling wholesale to groceries, convenience stores, and gas stations and part retail doughnut shop, complete with a neon light that periodically displays the seductive message, "Hot Doughnuts Now." This split personality is clearly reflected in Krispy Kreme's revenues, as the division between the two types of business in company-owned shops was an exact fifty-fifty in fiscal year 2013.

Krispy Kreme's original doughnuts—deep-fried in hot oil—have remained the same since the company's founding. Eaten while warm after the application of an assembly-line baptism of a molten glaze of confectioners' sugar, these creations provide a wondrously soft textural experience to the teeth and palate, along with delivering a dizzying burst of sweetness. An inventive writer once compared eating a Krispy Kreme glazed doughnut to a pleasant dream in which the slumberer imagines himself languorously and happily devouring his pillow.

Over forty doughnut varieties are available at Krispy Kreme, a number that always includes a few limited-time-only offerings. (The company at one point came out with a doughnut filled with Cheerwine-flavored crème. It was a huge hit in Salisbury, where the soft drink is bottled; see pages 177-79.) The array includes eclairs; fritters; iced, powdered, and glazed filled and unfilled doughnuts; twists; cake doughnuts of various flavors; crullers; and both glazed and cake doughnut holes.

Vernon Rudolph died in 1973, sixteen years before the 1989 establishment of the first Krispy Kreme operation devoted entirely to retail sales. Located on Greensboro's High Point Road, it provided a windowed vantage point from which customers could gaze mesmerized at doughnuts being produced on the automated assembly line. Although automation had pretty well taken over the doughnut-making process in 1963, customers hadn't previously been able to see it firsthand.

Hot doughnuts now!
KRISPY KREME

The iconic "Hot Doughnuts Now" light put in its first appearance in 1992. Less than twenty years later, mobile phones having pretty well taken over the world in the interim, Krispy Kreme launched its 2011 "Hot Light App" in response to customers' desire to receive notification when the doughnuts were hottest at their nearest Krispy Kreme location!

Although it wasn't until the 1990s that Krispy Kreme began to establish locations outside the southeastern United States, the company had expanded to thirty-eight states, coast to coast, by 2014. At that time, California led the nation with twenty-seven locations, while Florida was second with twenty-six stores and North Carolina third with twenty-four. Besides the stores Krispy Kreme operates in the United States and

Canada, it has locations in the United Kingdom, Australia, Lebanon, Turkey, the Dominican Republic, Kuwait, Mexico, Puerto Rico, Taiwan, South Korea, Malaysia, Thailand, Indonesia, the Philippines, Japan, China, the United Arab Emirates, Qatar, Saudi Arabia, Bahrain, Hong Kong, and Ethiopia.

Outside the United States, Krispy Kreme doughnuts are a novelty rather than a mainline snack food. That's part of the reason that some Canadian and overseas Krispy Kreme locations are considerably smaller than the traditional retail store/doughnut factory outlets that characterized the company for decades, and are supplied by centralized doughnut production facilities. Since this model has shown itself to be not only profitable but also easier to finance for franchisees, it's beginning to be used in a growing number of United States locations as well.

In Raleigh, what began as a challenge among ten friends has now turned into a fund-raising event with over eight thousand participants. The Krispy Kreme Challenge has as its mantra, "Twenty-four hundred calories, twelve doughnuts, five miles, one hour." Runners begin at the North Carolina State University bell tower and run two and a half miles through downtown Raleigh to the Krispy Kreme location at the corner of Peace and Person streets. There, they attempt to eat a dozen original glazed doughnuts, after which they run the two and a half miles back to the campus. The event is held in support of the North Carolina Children's Hospital, which received a donation of two hundred thousand dollars raised by individuals and teams during the 2014 event.

Perhaps the most entertaining and inspiring Krispy Kreme story I've heard involves Chris Rosati of Durham, who suffers from ALS, or Lou Gehrig's disease, a degenerative neuromuscular disorder that is ultimately fatal. While giving a talk at Durham Academy, Rosati told students about a fantasy in which he would hijack a Krispy Kreme delivery truck and drive around—maybe while having the cops chase him, for added drama—tossing out free doughnuts and good cheer to folks who needed a bright moment.

The students reacted so positively to the idea that Rosati became determined to make it happen, not by actually hijacking a truck but by getting Krispy Kreme involved as a co-conspirator. He wrote about the plan on a Facebook page he named "A Krispy Kreme Heist." Sure enough, it took only about eight hours before Krispy Kreme's marketing department got the word and offered him not a truck but a restored tour bus (with a driver), along with a thousand boxes of doughnuts to give away.

When the day for the "heist" arrived, Rosati had the driver head for Duke University Medical Center, where he delivered doughnuts and laughter first to a cancer treatment center, then to a bone marrow transplant facility and the clinic where he receives treatment for his ALS.

The next stop was Durham Academy, Rosati's alma mater, where four hundred highschoolers had been instructed to assemble outside on the sidewalk without being told why. When they saw the green polka-dotted bus with the bowtie Krispy Kreme logo pull up, they quickly figured out what was going on. Rosati told the students, many of them by now wearing Krispy Kreme's trademark paper hats, that it was important to work to make their dreams—"Even dumb ones like this"—come true. He explained that each of the students would get a doughnut, but that he also wanted some of them to take a box and go out into the community to give them away, just to produce smiles. "You get twelve chances in that box to make somebody happy," he said.

Rosati and his wife, Anna, plan to use a video of the "heist" to inspire others to engage in random acts of kindness through the couple's nonprofit Inspire Media Network. The Rosatis hope the nonprofit will eventually be able to help people fund uplifting projects of their own.

KRISPY KREME
DOUGHNUT CORP.

370 Knollwood Street #500
Winston-Salem, N.C. 27103
336-725-2981
www.krispykreme.com

Country HAM
BEYOND THE "DINOSAUR LEG"

Country ham, the American South's answer to the venerable dry-cured hams of Europe, can, at its best, possess a wonderfully complex taste and be deeply layered with flavor. Lesser versions, on the other hand, are mainly chewy and salty. We eat a lot of both kinds in North Carolina, although, like other Southerners, we generally eat less of the best and more of the middling variety, often between halves of a biscuit and often while we're behind the wheel of an automobile. Still, fast food has helped chisel out an enduring place for country ham in our food consciousness, reminding us to at least dream of doing better, if only on special occasions. After all, a man's reach should exceed his grasp.

To my taste, even so-so country ham is usually preferable to the other kind. Some "wet-cure" ham—injected with or soaked in brine containing sodium nitrate and flavorings—can be processed for sale in as little as twenty-four hours. It might aptly be called "city" ham, since most city (and now suburban) folks are simply in too much of a hurry. This shrink-wrapped, spiral-sliced, sugar-glazed version has a more forgiving texture, generally re-

quires only a relatively quick heating, and eliminates any worries about the ham's being too salty or about being able to carve it into paper-thin slices, which is de rigueur for country ham (although I'm not quite sure why, since plenty of people like thick, fried country ham steaks as a dinner entrée).

Much of the dry-cured country ham we North Carolinians consume has been pushed into being in more of a hurry, too. But even climate-controlled, fast-track country ham, which is mostly what North Carolina produces, is at least intended to approximate the flavor of old-style ham and the heirloom curing method that centers around time, patience, and tradition. A slice of real old-time country ham is supposed to somehow evoke the unchanging rhythm of life on the land and the changing of the seasons.

Part of the timeless seasonal ritual in pre-refrigeration days was the killing of hogs when cold weather arrived. Fresh hams set aside for curing were thickly coated with salt, sometimes mixed with brown sugar, and left to rest in this covering for about five weeks, during which time the temperature was expected to hold not far above freezing. The salt mixture, intended to draw around 25 percent of the moisture out of the meat, was then rinsed off, and the hams were wrapped in paper and hung in loosely woven cloth bags inside some sort of well-ventilated, unheated, and uncooled structure. There, in what is also called an "ambient" cure, they were exposed to plenty of fresh air and normal seasonal temperature and humidity fluctuations for another eight months to two years, or sometimes even longer. In Europe, which is much more laid-back about the passage of time than America, curing a ham has long been a more leisurely process. Bohemian folklore has it that a man blessed with the birth of a daughter during the winter might be expected to begin curing a ham that would be ready to serve on her wedding day.

Charlotte Observer food editor Kathleen Purvis explains, "The idea behind curing meat is simple: Salt draws out moisture. Without moisture, bacteria can't survive. The trick is to remove enough moisture to keep the meat from spoiling while leaving enough to make the meat palatable. These days, since people want sweeter ham, they lower the salt and increase the sugar as much as possible, while still making the ham safe to eat. The most the law will allow is 6 parts salt to 1 part sugar."

Incidentally, the phrase *sugar-cured ham* is misleading. Only salt really cures a ham; sugar merely flavors the meat.

In a July 2009 *New York Times* article, noted food author Harold McGee, who writes often about the chemistry of food and cooking, explained the process inherent in the time-intensive ambient curing process: "It takes many months for muscle enzymes to break down flavorless proteins into savory amino acids, odorless fats into aromatic fragments, and for all these chemical bits and pieces to interact and generate new layers of flavor. And it takes months for meat to lose moisture and develop a density of flavor and texture."

And if the conditions are just right, what might one expect from this unhurried process? McGee answered with questions of his own: "Have you ever placed a vanishingly thin morsel of rosy meat on your tongue and had it fill your mouth with deepest porkiness, or the aroma of tropical fruits, or caramel, or chocolate? Or all of the above?"

American country hams generally do not attract the critical acclaim or exalted price of their European predecessors, which is no big deal to most of us and probably even a source of perverse pride. From the beginning, the demands and hardships of settlement in the New World made ham curing more a practical necessity than an art, and the prevailing Southern weather forced some of the nuances of the curing process to be sacrificed. Spain and Italy, in particular, produce artisanal air-cured hams that set the standard for the rest of the world and can sell for thirty to a hundred dollars per pound. But you really can't compare our dry-cured hams to theirs. The subtly flavored *jamons iberico* and prosciuttos are typically aged in summer temperatures that run from ten to thirty degrees below those of the American South. The more intense heat here gives our country hams a considerably

No matter the time of day, country ham always goes well with grits and red-eye gravy.
CARO-MI DINING ROOM

stronger flavor. Heat speeds up enzyme activity and produces a more robust, pungent flavor—more of a country twang, if you will. In our new, raw, proudly rough-and-tumble country, that may have been considered a mark of distinction, rather than a drawback. Our weather has also made ham curing much more unpredictable. Producers have sometimes lost up to 30 percent of their old-style cured hams during a season.

If Southern country hams thus evolved over time into slightly cruder and less expensive regional products compared to European air-cured hams, as McGee maintained, they were still too high on the hog for many settlers and small farmers, including some of those who produced them. My late mother, who grew up on a tiny eastern North Carolina tobacco farm during the 1920s and 1930s, recalled that while her family raised hogs and cured hams, she and her nine siblings seldom got to sample them. "We kept sausage and side meat," she reminisced, "but Daddy had to sell all the hams he cured to scrape together enough cash for us to be able to buy staples like flour and sugar."

Even among those who could afford to eat their own cured hams or to purchase hams from someone else, they were still considered holiday or special-occasion fare. While European dry-cured hams are often consumed uncooked and in small servings, antipasto-style, most American country hams have traditionally been soaked and simmered to varying degrees (to leech out some of the saltiness), then baked with a fruit or sugar glaze for serving at gatherings. This is changing. Most American producers have transitioned into pre-sliced, packaged country ham, the aims being to help consumers with ease of cooking and to supply restaurants with smaller portions that can be prepared and served in creative ways.

The great bulk of country ham is cured in Kentucky, Tennessee, North Carolina, Virginia, and Missouri. Inevitably, it's a declining enterprise. In today's fast-paced, activity-laden lifestyle, most families don't have the time, inclination, or know-how to deal with preparing a whole dry-cured ham, which many producers privately call a "dinosaur leg." The number of country ham producers in the United States has declined in recent decades from several thousand to around fifty. North Carolina has only one remaining true climate-cured country ham producer, A. B. Vannoy Hams of West Jefferson, a company that doesn't get nearly the acclaim it deserves, despite its practice of air-curing high-quality hams for nine months to two years. That's at least partially because the company wasn't certified and inspected to sell outside the state until 2009.

Based on published reviews, the most highly rated country hams seem to come from Kentucky, followed by Tennessee, North Carolina, and Virginia. Surprisingly, considering our dearth of old-fashioned ambient-cure houses, North Carolina actually led the nation in the production of country ham until recently, and now runs a close second to Tennessee. However, with the single exception of A. B. Vannoy, all the Tar Heel firms employ some form of accelerated dry curing, in which temperature and humidity are artificially and closely controlled to simulate changing seasonal conditions, thereby producing an "aged" ham in a span of as little as three months.

It should be said, though, that the technique of accelerated aging has made progress in terms of quality. Some North Carolina quick-cure producers age their products four to six months—a bit longer than the minimum—and a couple of those have received accolades in national publication taste tests. So has at least one brand from a well-known south-side Virginia ham house that uses quick-curing methods in addition to longer-term climate aging (see page 156).

In most country-ham-producing states, cured hams are usually hickory-smoked after all or a major portion of the aging process is complete. The smoking darkens and flavors the hams, although it has nothing to do with actually curing the meat. Some companies employ high-tech methods of producing and circulating smoke around the hams, while others simply build a low fire in a fireplace, try to keep the overall temperature in the smokehouse around ninety degrees, and let the smoke do its work. For some reason, smoking is not an ordinary part of the country ham curing process in North Carolina, although at least one producer, Johnston County Hams of Smithfield, offers a hickory-smoked ham that has garnered favorable reviews.

Although country hams are cured as whole joints of meat, they aren't mainly marketed that way any longer. Fewer than seven million whole country hams are sold each year in the United States. That means a significant percentage of North Carolina's fast-track country ham is sold in pre-sliced, vacuum-packaged form, some to individual consumers in grocery stores and even more to restaurants and through institutional channels, where it is served most often as a breakfast meat, alongside eggs, grits, and red-eye gravy.

And that brings me to the huge role of breakfast sandwiches in the country ham story. They're responsible not only for popularizing country ham among a much wider demographic than just the aging consumers who comprise much of the market for whole, traditionally cured hams, but also for absorbing a huge portion of the production of pre-sliced ham. For example, breakfast sandwiches—including country ham biscuits—account for nearly half the total sales at Hardee's, the North Carolina–born fast-food chain with thousands of locations across the South and Midwest.

The ham biscuit is the star at Hardee's but has achieved lesser, if still respectable, fame at places like Bojangles' and McDonald's. One blogger on GrubGrade, an Internet site devoted to reviews of the fast-food industry, wrote, "Hardee's has created a masterpiece that is now in my top 5 all-time sandwiches. While not the best country ham I have ever had, it easily blows every other fast food pork product out of the water." Perhaps country ham that rates as "good enough" is sufficient as a filling for a Hardee's biscuit, which, the blogger enthused, "is like a dense, buttery pillow sent by the gods."

North Carolinians do love their ham biscuits. Consider the case of Biscuitville, the Greensboro-headquartered breakfast and lunch chain that began in Burlington in the mid-1960s. It started as a couple of bread and milk stores that sold takeout pizza more or less as an afterthought, then morphed into several stand-alone pizza restaurants named Pizzaville. Deciding to put his idle pizza ovens to use during the pre-lunch hours, owner Maurice Jennings started baking fresh breakfast biscuits, which were originally sold with a trip to a "jelly bar" thrown in. Customers quickly made it clear they wanted meat, not jelly, in their biscuits. When country ham was introduced as a biscuit filling, the popularity of the place skyrocketed, and the pizza service evaporated. Today, Biscuitville has dozens of restaurants in North Carolina and Virginia and goes through more than four thousand pounds of country ham per week.

Confronting the declining market for whole hams, old-fashioned dry-cure ham houses have joined the quick-cure operations in branching heavily into vacuum-packaged country ham, not only center-cut and biscuit slices but also boneless ham sections of various sizes. Offering customers a convenient bypass around the intimidating eighteen-plus hours of soaking and cooking required for whole country hams, several top-rated ambient-cure operations have also begun shipping fully cooked whole country hams—for a hefty price.

Competing sociological trends make the continued desirability of country ham and other traditional foods uncertain. On one hand, it's hard to deny that most of us are too busy and distracted to do much more than get a country ham breakfast fix once in a while.

And yet the popularity of TV cooking shows and cooking blogs, the ability to obtain high-end food products via Internet mail order, and other factors offer a glimmer of optimism to those trying to maintain the craft of country ham curing. Interest in artisanal and locally sourced foods is also growing rapidly across the restaurant scene, as is a certain fascination with anything having to do with pigs and cured pork.

Foodies being what they are, I believe a reverence for traditional foodways and a sense of adventure will always lead new devotees to test their cooking chops with an entire old-fashioned country ham.

Here's a little of what they'll need to know.

SLICED HAM: SLOW FRYING VERSUS QUICK FRYING

If you're one of those people who think an apt definition of eternity is "two people and a ham," or if you don't think your sizable holiday crowd could possibly consume an entire country ham, you're better off frying packaged slices. You can even do this to fill a platter for your holiday table, particularly if you have a chafing dish suitable for keeping the slices slightly warm and moistened with red-eye gravy (see page 147).

Some cooks suggest heating slices—enough to cover the bottom of a large skillet—for around twenty minutes at low temperature. Cover the pan and cook the ham slowly enough for the juices to collect, rather than solidifying into a crust. Turn the slices halfway through the cooking time.

While this slow-frying works fine, I believe you will produce even more succulent fried ham slices with a noticeably lighter, more yielding "bite" by cooking them more quickly at a higher temperature. I'm a fan of preheating the skillet for a couple of minutes over medium heat, then tossing in no more than two center-cut slices and cooking them for exactly forty-five seconds per side, and no more. If the ham is trimmed lean, you can grease the skillet with a tablespoon or so of butter as it preheats, but if the slices have visible fat, don't bother.

RED-EYE GRAVY

Remove the slices immediately, reduce the heat slightly, and pour several tablespoons of black coffee into the pan, along with a quarter-cup or so of water. Use a nylon or rubber spatula to deglaze the thin, brown "ham crust" from the bottom of the skillet so it blends with the liquid. When the liquid returns to a simmer, place the slices back into the skillet for thirty seconds on each side, then remove them to a plate, spoon some of the red-eye gravy over the meat (and maybe over some accompanying hominy grits), and have at it. Incidentally, the grits will be much richer and creamier if you cook them in milk, rather than water.

BAKING SLICED HAM

You can bake packaged country ham slices in the oven by sprinkling them with a little brown sugar, wrapping them in aluminum foil, and placing the foil packet in an ovenproof baking dish to catch any wayward juices. Bake for a half-hour at 350 degrees.

ALL IN: COOKING A WHOLE HAM

If you're going to cook an entire country ham, you'll either be simmering it in a pot of water on the stovetop; braising it in a roaster in the oven, covered with liquid (this process is also known as pot-roasting); or baking it in the oven, covered with an aluminum foil tent. First, though, you'll have to soak it. Unless you elect a longer initial soaking time, you'll probably end up choosing simmering or braising, rather than baking.

Once the ham is cooked according to your chosen method, you'll let it cool, then remove the rind (outer skin) and most of the fat, using a sharp, thin-bladed knife.

One final, optional step will be to score the remaining fat (mostly for the sake of appearance), apply some sort of sweet or fruity glaze, and do a quick, final baking to caramelize the fat and glaze. This is not absolutely necessary, and since most cooks recommend thoroughly chilling the ham once it's cooked so that it's easier to cut into thin slices, you may choose to dispense with this step. It all depends on what kind of splash you want to make in the presentation of the ham at the table.

PREPPING AND SOAKING

A great deal of moisture was lost during the curing and aging process, so success in cooking a whole ham begins with rehydrating the cured meat, adding back the lost moisture.

Before starting the rehydrating process, remove the protective paper. If mold is on the skin (rind) of the ham, don't worry, as this is perfectly normal and actually enhances flavor. Simply scrub it off with a plastic scrubber or a stiff brush under warm running water. Next, cut about three inches off the hock, which is the narrow end of the ham. You can do this yourself with a hand saw, or you can get your butcher to do it. Don't throw away the ham hock, since it's great for seasoning beans or greens!

You'll need to totally submerge the ham in unheated tap water, either in a cooler or a large pot with a cover. Most experts recommend a soaking of at least twelve hours, with the container left outside unless it's below freezing. Some maintain the ham will be better and the cooked meat more moist—and less salty—if you soak it for two, three, or four days, changing the water at twelve-hour intervals, every morning and evening. Add enough ice to the soaking water to keep the ham cool if it's hot outside.

BRAISING (POT-ROASTING)

Use this in-the-oven variation of the method for simmering country ham if you don't have a large enough stockpot with a lid but do own a big roaster. Place the ham, skin side up, in an open roaster that's deep enough for the water to completely cover the ham. Preheat the oven to 350 degrees, add hot water to within two inches of the top of the roaster, and put the roaster in the oven. After cooking for ten minutes, reduce the heat to 250 degrees and continue cooking for twenty minutes per pound. Let the ham cool in the roaster before handling.

You can combine any of the following optional ingredients with water to produce enough liquid to cover the ham: a cup of molasses, a sixty-four-ounce bottle of apple juice, a cup of vinegar and a cup of brown sugar, a sixty-four-ounce bottle of cola, or a quart of bourbon. Some people use the following, blended with a quart of apple cider: a medium-sized quartered onion studded with cloves, a dozen whole black peppercorns, half a dozen allspice berries, a bay leaf, and a quartered apple.

SIMMERING ON THE STOVETOP

After soaking the ham for at least twelve hours, drain and replace the water. Place the pot containing the ham and fresh water on the stove and bring it to a boil, then reduce the heat to simmer and cover the pot. Simmer the ham for twenty minutes per pound, plus an extra thirty minutes for good measure. It's important that you don't allow the water to come to a full boil, but just a simmer. Add hot water as needed to keep the ham totally covered. You can add any of the above-mentioned ingredients to the water.

Once it's done, let the ham cool in the cooking liquid before handling it.

BAKING THE WHOLE HAM

Choose this method only if you've given the ham an extra-long soaking. Remove the rind and most of the fat before cooking. Most cooks score the remaining fat to help it render as it bakes. Place the ham fat side up in a large roasting pan. Preheat the oven to 400 degrees. Completely cover the ham with a tent of aluminum foil, pour a quart of water or apple juice into the pan, and place it in the oven. Cook for an hour and a half, turn the ham, and reduce the heat to 325 degrees. Cook another three hours, turning the ham again after an hour and a half at the lower temperature. Let the ham cool in the cooking liquid for thirty minutes before the final glazing, or skip the glazing and refrigerate the ham until it's well chilled to make thin slicing easier.

THE WRAP-COOKING METHOD

My friend Jack Betts, a retired *Charlotte Observer* associate editor who was a cheerleader with me at UNC–Chapel Hill, has a neighbor in Patrick County, Virginia, who claims to possess the world's best and easiest way to cook a country ham. Former Virginia legislator and Patrick County manager Barnie K. Day readily admits he stole this recipe.

After cutting off the hock, submerge the ham in fresh, clean water in a pot (with a lid) that will hold enough liquid to cover the ham by three or four inches. Bring the pot to a boil and immediately remove it from the stove, leaving it covered. Put a couple of inches of newspapers over and under the pot, then wrap the entire cooking vessel in something to help insulate it—a sleeping bag, a lounge cushion, a big piece of foam cut for that purpose, or anything else that will hold in the heat. Tie the insulation securely around the pot with heavy twine or baling wire and leave it alone for a full twelve hours—preferably overnight, so you won't be tempted to peek. Remove the wrap, take the ham out of the pot, and put it in a large roaster or baking pan. Be cautious during this step, since the water will be too hot for your hands; you'll probably need heavy rubber gloves or a couple of large meat forks to transfer the ham. Let the meat cool, then remove the rind and most of the fat. Score the remaining encasing fat into a diamond pattern and rub a cup of white sugar into the scored area. Bake the ham at 275 degrees for two hours. Let it cool completely or refrigerate it before slicing, so you can produce those pretty, thin slices that peel so nicely off the knife in front of your guests.

GLAZING AND BAKING

If you simmered the ham in a covered pot or braised it in a roaster, this is a potential next step. After removing the rind and scoring the fat, you can put a glaze on the ham and brown it for presentation, although this makes for a rather complex carving job at the table. Below are suggestions for some traditional glazes, courtesy of Tripp Country Hams of Brownsville, Tennessee, and the Loveless Café of Nashville, Tennessee.

PINEAPPLE-BROWN SUGAR GLAZE

Mix a small can of crushed pineapple with two-thirds of a cup of brown sugar until the mixture becomes smooth. Pour and brush it over the fat, then garnish the ham's surface with sliced pineapple and cherries. Bake at 400 degrees for twenty minutes until the surface is golden brown.

HONEY GLAZE

Combine one-fourth cup of orange juice, one-fourth cup of honey, and a teaspoon of

yellow mustard. Pour and brush it over the ham, then put the ham under the broiler for ten to fifteen minutes.

BROWN SUGAR AND SHERRY GLAZE

Sprinkle the cored fat with ground cloves. Combine two-thirds of a cup of brown sugar with a third of a cup of sherry. Pour and brush the glaze over the scored fat, then bake at 425 degrees for ten to fifteen minutes until the exterior is nicely browned.

GINGER ALE AND BROWN SUGAR GLAZE

After removing the rind and scoring the fat, place the ham in a roaster and bake at 325 degrees for an hour, basting often with a mixture of one cup each of ginger ale and ham stock. Remove the ham and cover the fat with a glaze of a cup of brown sugar, half a cup of molasses, four tablespoons of flour, a tablespoon of dry mustard, and two tablespoons of water. Garnish the diamond-shaped sections of scored fat with whole cloves. Return the uncovered ham to the oven and bake thirty more minutes at 325 degrees.

CRANBERRY GLAZE

Stud the diamond-shaped sections of scored fat with whole cloves. Combine two cans of jellied cranberry sauce and a cup of brown sugar. Spread half of this mixture over the ham and bake at 350 degrees for thirty minutes until well browned. Heat the remaining cranberry sauce–sugar mixture and serve as a sauce over the cooked ham.

BOURBON GLAZE

Combine a quarter-cup of real maple syrup, half a cup of brown sugar, a tablespoon of dry mustard, and a cup of bourbon. Pour and spread it over the ham fat, put the ham in the oven, and bake at 350 degrees for one hour.

CARVING A COUNTRY HAM

You'll likely want to carve a glazed country ham at the table (or at a carving station at a buffet dinner) to put on a bit of a show. If you're up for it, here's how it's done. The following tips come from the Loveless Café of Nashville, Tennessee.

A country ham has two flat sides and two curved sides. Using a sharp, long-bladed knife, trim some slices horizontally from the bottom of the less curved side so that the ham can sit flat on a cutting board or platter. Stand the ham on the newly flattened side and carve downward toward the bone through the more curved side. Do not carve horizontally (or with the grain of the meat), but rather cut down, across the grain. Begin near the hock by cutting vertically through to the bone, then

move up three or four inches and make another slightly diagonal cut, removing the meat between the two cuts to give you room to work. Slicing paper-thin slices (or as thin as you're able to manage if the ham is still warm from the glazing process), work toward the large end of the ham. Keep the knife inclined at such an angle that you are eventually cutting thin slices six to eight inches long.

FEATURE ATTRACTIONS

A. B. VANNOY HAMS

Byron and Nancy Jordan pay homage to traditional pork in a couple of different ways up in the Ashe County mountain community of West Jefferson. They serve authentic, wood-cooked, whole-hog barbecue at their restaurant, Smoky Mountain Barbecue, and sell old-style, climate-cured country ham in their side business, A. B. Vannoy Hams. The busy barbecue restaurant serves as the retail center for the hams.

The Jordans bought this venerable family ham-curing operation as a second business from founder A. B. "Burl" Vannoy's daughter in 1984. The elder Vannoy began producing air-cured country hams in the 1930s. His market gradually spread eastward across North Carolina and down into the Charlotte area. The Jordans still use the founder's original ham house and his family's old-fashioned curing methods, producing country hams that

they are fond of saying have only four ingredients: "salt, brown sugar, mountain air, and time." Nothing injected. Absolutely no artificial preservatives such as nitrites or nitrates.

Nancy Jordan runs the business most of the time, handling the inspection, weighing, order filling, and shipping. She wonders about the number of young customers coming along who will buy hams. "Our hams aren't as salty as some, and younger people are becoming more familiar with bold flavor through being exposed to more traditional cured meats these days, so it isn't so much the taste issue that concerns me," Nancy says. "But when it comes to purchasing a whole ham, they're hesitant. We have to educate them that a whole ham isn't just one meal. It may turn into thirty meals, with little slices and bits tucked away in Ziploc bags in the freezer, ready to emerge at a moment's notice to provide a quick entrée or some wonderful seasoning, or to furnish an effective topping or garnish. And of course now we can sell them shelf-stable, packaged

ham slices to help them sort of ease into the process."

The Jordans benefit from the tourist traffic circulating through West Jefferson. Word of mouth is a big part of their marketing approach, along with their website and their relatively recent ability to ship ham anywhere in the United States. They've noticed that more mature customers with European backgrounds and tastes have a special appreciation for their longer-aged hams—the ones cured for a couple of years. This is also the type of ham they typically sell in small, prepackaged quantities to high-end restaurants, where it typically shows up as a flavoring or layering ingredient, rather than an entrée.

It's fitting that West Jefferson is home to North Carolina's last remaining cheese factory, considering that Ashe County used to have a dozen cheese producers. Likewise, the town hosts this, the state's last air-cured country ham operation, whereas the county once boasted five other ham houses. Business owners here and elsewhere became leery of dealing with knotty state regulations and tying up their money for months in aging a product that fewer people seem to want to buy. Only a thin slice of the population seems to appreciate the difference between a grocery-store ham and one that's been cured and aged, as the Jordans' hams are, from nine months to two years.

On the other hand, taste for the product isn't disappearing. A lot of possible future customers enjoy country ham breakfast sandwiches on a regular basis; there's revived interest in every aspect of regional and local heritage; TV food shows are increasingly hungry for feature material; and the fascination with slowly made local foods is definitely on the rise. It's enough to make an artisanal food craftsman want to stay in the game, at least until there's more clarity in the changing market.

So the Jordans are still, Byron jokes, "hamming it up." The couple buys around sixteen hundred hams each year from Midwestern hog producers. Most of the work is concentrated in January, when their workers coat some forty-two thousand pounds of meat with salt and brown sugar, leaving the hams in the curing mixture for thirty-six to thirty-nine days as they "take the salt." Then the workers rinse the salt off, wrap the hams in brown paper, and hang them in cloth nets in the old upstairs aging room. Dangling from the original heavy wooden beams, the hams are exposed to fresh air pulled through the open windows by ventilating fans. They hang there for the next nine months to two years.

The hottest months—June, July, and August—are when the heat really activates the salt, causing it to be drawn from the cut surface of the hock, where most of it was applied, throughout the meat. The salt drives out the moisture, which in turn stops the growth of bacteria.

A really hot summer often produces stronger flavors in the meat and can cause the hams to become too dry. Too much rainy weather increases the mold on the outside of the hams, which is entirely harmless but often worries customers who don't realize they can simply wash it off. The weather is as inconsistent and unpredictable as customers' tastes.

But in the end, here's what the Jordans and their customers are hoping for. By October, the blade of an ice pick inserted through the rind and deep into a ham will emerge carrying a faint but incomparably rich, sweet aroma that will make anyone's mouth begin to water.

A. B. Vannoy Hams is a small concern, relatively speaking, so it hasn't attracted the accolades won by some other country ham producers. But I've cooked the Jordans' whole hams and fried up a lot of their slices, and in my opinion, the company's hams are among the tastiest air-cured hams available.

The Jordans suggest soaking a ham for two twelve-hour cycles (changing the water after the first cycle), then simmering it in a large stockpot or roaster for fifteen minutes per pound to an internal temperature of 160 degrees. After the soaking water is poured off, they recommend covering the ham with apple juice, then adding a cup of brown sugar, a pint of pineapple juice, and twelve whole cloves before simmering.

The couple offers another handy tip. Slices from a whole ham can be kept in a plastic tub in the refrigerator for up to four months if they're covered by cooking oil. Simply wash off the oil under warm water and dry with paper towels to ready the slices for the frying pan.

A. B. VANNOY HAMS

205 Buck Mountain Road
West Jefferson, N.C. 28694
336-246-3319 (ham house) or 336-246-6818 (Smoky Mountain Barbecue)
abvannoyhams.com

CARO-MI DINING ROOM

The Caro-Mi Dining Room in Polk County may be the only remaining restaurant in North Carolina where old-fashioned, air-cured country ham is featured as a dinner entrée.

The Tryon restaurant buys whole hams from A. B. Vannoy in West Jefferson, cuts them into center slices on a band saw in the kitchen, fries the ham steaks on a flat-top grill (being careful not to overcook them), and serves the richly flavored meat with grits and red-eye gravy. Neither the whole hams nor the slices are soaked or simmered in any way—the slices aren't even returned to the red-eye gravy for a few moments before being plated—so there is no attempt to reduce the saltiness. Owner Dane Stafford says he warns

customers that if they aren't used to country ham, they will definitely find this entrée salty, and that if they're concerned about that, they might want to order something else.

The Caro-Mi has been showcasing country ham in pretty much this exact way since 1945. Since 1990, it's been doing it under the Stafford family, who took over from the original owners. Through the decades, a steady stream of customers has continued to make its way to the rustic restaurant—by way of a scenic covered bridge across the Pacolet River—to enjoy the Caro-Mi's signature presentation.

Mountain trout, fried chicken, fried shrimp and/or scallops, fried flounder, grilled mahi-mahi, and pan-sautéed chicken livers are the menu alternatives for those who are skittish about the straightforward, full-bore country ham.

The Caro-Mi's iconic briny, vinegary slaw and macaroni salad are two longtime specialties that always show up at the table. Green beans, fried apples, and biscuits put in appearances as well.

The Caro-Mi's original owners were from Miami, Florida; the restaurant's name is a combination of *Carolina* and *Miami*. Reservations are encouraged but not required. Checks are accepted but credit and debit cards are not.

CARO-MI DINING ROOM

3231 U.S. 176 West
Tryon, N.C. 28782
828-859-5200
www.caro-mi.com
Dinner, Wednesday through Saturday

The Caro-Mi Dining Room enjoys a picturesque location outside Tryon, in the southern North Carolina foothills.
CARO-MI DINING ROOM

OTHER LOCATIONS FOR ORDERING COUNTRY HAM

THE FOLLOWING country ham suppliers—traditional air-cured and accelerated-cure, climate-controlled operations, in both North Carolina and other states—have all received high ratings in national publications or at industry competitions.

TRADITIONAL AIR-CURED COUNTRY HAMS

BENTON'S SMOKY MOUNTAIN COUNTRY HAMS

2603 U.S. 411
North Madisonville, Tenn. 37354
423-442-5003
bentonscountryhams2.com

BROADBENT'S

257 Mary Blue Road
Kuttawa, Ky. 42055
800-841-2202
www.broadbenthams.com

COL. BILL NEWSOM'S AGED KENTUCKY COUNTRY HAM

208 East Main Street
Princeton, Ky. 42445
270-365-2482
www.newsomscountryham.com

FATHER'S COUNTRY HAMS

6323 Ky. 81

P.O. Box 99

Bremen, Ky. 42325

877-525-4267 or 270-525-3554

www.fatherscountryhams.com

S. WALLACE EDWARDS & SONS

P.O. Box 25

Surry, Va. 23883

800-222-4267 or 800-290-9213

www.edwardsvaham.com

Note: This company sells both bone-in Wigwam country ham, aged ten to twelve months, and Edwards Virginia Traditions ham, aged four to six months.

ACCELERATED-CURE, CLIMATE-CONTROLLED COUNTRY HAMS

The following sell hams aged from three to six months.

BURGER'S SMOKEHOUSE

32819 Mo. 87

California, Mo. 65018

800-345-5185

www.smokehouse.com

CLIFTY FARM COUNTRY MEATS

P.O. Box 1146

Paris, Tenn. 38242

800-486-4267

www.cliftyfarm.com

GOODNIGHT BROTHERS COUNTRY HAM

372 Industrial Park Drive

Boone, N.C. 28607

828-264-8892

www.goodnightbrothers.com

HARPER'S COUNTRY HAMS

2955 U.S. 51 North

P.O. Box 122

Clinton, Ky. 42031

888-427-7377

www.hamtastic.com

JOHNSTON COUNTY HAMS

204 North Brightleaf Boulevard

Smithfield, N.C. 27577

919-934-8054

www.countrycuredhams.com

TRIPP COUNTRY HAMS

P.O. Box 527

Brownsville, Tenn. 38012

800-471-9814

www.countryhams.com

Awash IN SAUCE

I have long observed that North Carolina is pretty well awash in its own bottled sauces.

In the same way that every good cook is told by his friends, "You ought to open a restaurant," every good cook who likes to experiment with sauces eventually comes up with one that leads friends and neighbors to say, "You ought to bottle that."

Not many bottled sauces make it, since the process is one continuous battle for shelf space in stores—space that must often be purchased, at least by lesser-known sauce manufacturers. However, it is possible to start small; to show up at scores of sauce contests, in-store demonstrations, and food expos to build the product's reputation; to set up an online marketing site; and to gradually work one's way up to the big-time goal of being displayed in grocery stores. Compared to the difficulty of launching other food-related enterprises, marketing sauces is still among the low-hanging fruit.

North Carolina's rich barbecue tradition, and specifically its two distinctive regional styles of barbecue sauce, are, ironically, not well represented in the selection of bottled sauces available across the state. Commercial versions of mild, sweet, tomato-kissed "Lexington dip"—the signature dressing of the Piedmont's pork shoulder barbecue—can be found only sporadically outside the premises of barbecue restaurants, most of which do sell their own particular sauce on-site. Eastern North Carolina vinegar-based sauces are easier to find in chain stores, particularly in the coastal plain, and easier yet to find in small, local grocery markets—the sorts of places that carry old-fashioned hard Christmas candy, for example, or have their own butcher counters.

But North Carolina is inevitably becoming a "red" state in terms of bottled barbecue sauce. Many of the people who have moved here from all over the country, bringing their own tastes and expectations, wouldn't even consider purchasing our native vinegar-pepper sauce or light tomato Lexington dip. The generic, go-to barbecue sauce in nearly all regions of the state is, instead, a thick ketchup-based sauce, often heavily flavored with molasses, that was once chiefly identified with the barbecue centers of Kansas City and Memphis.

This is the sauce most Americans—and now most North Carolinians—call to mind when they think of barbecued ribs, barbecued chicken, or even pulled pork.

Quite a few North Carolina restaurants are also blurring the lines when it comes to barbecue sauce. Charlie Carden of Charlie's Barbecue and Grille in Clayton cooks his barbecued pork, beef brisket, and chicken in an electrically fired wood smoker, rather than a traditional pit. And he likes cross-pollination when it comes to sauce styles. "I've sampled every type of North Carolina barbecue, and I like 'em all. So we take the vinegar sauce of the east, the tomato-based sauce from around Lexington, and the thicker, redder sauces of western North Carolina and sort of combine the best of each," says Charlie. "What we end up with is sort of like a hybrid car."

An increasing number of other barbecue eateries, most of which use the smoker cooking style imported from the Midwest and West, also feature sauces other than the previously typical vinegar-pepper and Lexington-style dressings. Nearly all these places confirm that a thick, sweet, red sauce is their top seller, and a surprising number also offer as an option the sweet, yellow mustard-based sauce more properly identified with South Carolina. (You can also find this mustard barbecue sauce in a growing number of groceries.) There are really only four major styles of barbecue sauce to be found in the entire country: vinegar-pepper, Lexington dip, mustard-based, and thick tomato. On many barbecue restaurant tables across North Carolina, you're likely to find all four of them these days, with no particular preference accorded to our own native sauces. You're likely to discover a larger grocery-store selection of South Carolina mustard sauce than eastern vinegar-pepper sauce and Lexington dip combined. The vast majority of stuff on the shelves is thick, red, and fairly sweet.

Below are descriptions of some of North Carolina's premier sauces—be they of the barbecue, hot, or seasoning variety—along with a recipe featuring a tasty seasoning sauce.

BOB GARNER'S SIMPLE ZING WINGS

salt
1 dozen chicken wing portions
½ cup plus 3 tablespoons Capsicana Zing Gourmet Sauce (page 173), divided
½ cup Worcestershire sauce (I prefer Lea & Perrins)
4 tablespoons melted butter

Salt wings lightly and let sit for a few minutes. Whisk together ½ cup of the Zing, Worcestershire, and butter. In a medium-sized mixing bowl, toss wings with Zing mixture until well coated. Bake at 325 degrees for 45 minutes to 1 hour until wings are golden brown and tender. Remove wings and toss with remaining 3 tablespoons of Zing to coat before serving.

North Carolina's most common barbecue sauce is now a thick, red mixture once more closely associated with the barbecue traditions of the American heartland.
Mike Oniffrey

FEATURE ATTRACTIONS

BARBECUE SAUCES

SCOTT'S BARBECUE SAUCE

Scott's is one of the few eastern sauces you are likely to find in a grocery.

Adam Scott, a black minister, got into the barbecue business in Goldsboro in 1917. He built his first barbecue restaurant by enclosing the back porch of his home in 1931, mainly so customers wouldn't have to queue up in his yard for so long while waiting for some barbecue to take home. Ironically, the restaurant served only whites to begin with, while blacks had to settle for takeout. Later expansions of the restaurant featured separate white and black dining rooms until the federal courts intervened in the 1960s.

Scott said the original recipe for his fiery eastern-style vinegar-pepper sauce came to him in a dream. He served that version on his take-home barbecue and at his restaurant until the mid-1940s. At that time, Adam's son, A. Martel Scott, tweaked the ingredients of the sugar-free, fat-free mixture and obtained a patent on the sauce.

Scott's Barbecue Sauce

Responding to a telephone tip, police once discovered a late-night burglar at Scott's Barbecue hiding in a nearly full barrel of the caustic sauce. They hauled the robber out of the drum and threw him in a jail cell without benefit of a shower, so he spent the night literally marinating in the stuff. When Martel Scott showed up at the jail the next day, he told the authorities he wasn't going to press charges, since the unfortunate would-be thief had "already suffered enough."

Mindy Heiferling of *Food & Wine* magazine described Scott's Barbecue Sauce as "a hot, thin-bodied, tangy sauce that lingers on the tongue." Another expert said it's a "thin vinegary sauce with heat, like a hot pepper sauce. It's good on anything—that's if you can stand the fire."

You'll find this quintessential eastern sauce—with its familiar yellow and red label emblazoned with the motto, "It's the best ye ever tasted"—in most grocery stores in eastern and central North Carolina.

SCOTT'S BARBECUE SAUCE

P.O. Drawer 1380

Goldsboro, N.C. 27533

800-734-7282 or 919-734-0711

www.scottsbarbecuesauce.com

GEORGE'S BARBECUE SAUCE

George's, bottled in Nashville, near Rocky Mount, is representative of the basting sauces commonly used at many eastern North Carolina whole-hog barbecues, or pig pickings. It's a vinegar-pepper-salt blend that also has a little sugar and some tomato purée added, like many of the finishing sauces mopped over roasted whole hogs before serving. The overall flavor profile still says eastern North Carolina, but George's sauce wouldn't be tossed out the back door of most Piedmont barbecue restaurants either.

Many amateur pit masters tell me George's is the commercial sauce that comes closest in overall taste to what they concoct at home for whole-pig roasts, at which they usually serve the pork "pulled" or in hunks. If they're planning to use a cleaver to turn the pig into chopped barbecue, most are more likely to omit the sugar and tomato and go with a more straightforward vinegar-pepper recipe.

George Stallings of Rocky Mount got the enterprise started when he developed the original sauce in his home kitchen. He used it on his own barbecue and gave bottles to friends and relatives. By the mid-1970s, he had a small but solid business going, even though he cooked some of his first batches in a garage with a dirt floor.

Beth Chappell of Nashville bought the business from Stallings in 1992. The still-modest George's production facility now turns out some thirty-five hundred bottles of barbecue sauce each working day, making the mixture one of the most popular in the Carolinas. Every bottle is still labeled, filled, capped, and packed by hand.

Inevitably, George's also produces a thick red version for ribs and chicken, along with a

George's "Hot" Barbecue Sauce; there is also a milder "Original" version.

hot version with twice the heat of the original recipe.

GEORGE'S SAUCES

1173 Womble Road
Nashville, N.C. 27856
252-459-3084
www.georgesbbqsauce.com

BONE SUCKIN' SAUCE

Sandi Ford of Raleigh's Ford's Gourmet Foods, the sister-in-law of sauce developer Phil Ford, is responsible for naming this enormously popular and incredibly well-marketed red sauce. The name reportedly arose as her admission to sucking the last bit of sauce and flavor off pork and chicken bones.

The family's gourmet and specialty foods business, located at the State Farmers' Market in Raleigh, was already well established in 1992 when it partnered with Phil—who wasn't previously involved in the firm—to bring his sauce to market some five years after he began trying to re-create his mother's recipe. Things started to take off in earnest when the first Bone Suckin' Sauce won the North Carolina Battle of the Sauces in March 1984.

Today, the original sauce is just one of

a wide range of Ford's Gourmet Foods Bone Suckin' products, including a South Carolina–style mustard sauce, a steak sauce, and others. The firm now ships its sauce line to nearly sixty countries, with 20 percent of its business coming from exports.

The original sauce, which is a bit thinner than many other red barbecue sauces and contains Liquid Smoke, is said to be a favorite of President Obama. Both the original recipe and various succeeding sauces have won a pile of awards, including number-one ratings from both *Newsweek* and *Food & Wine*. But it is at least worth noting with curiosity that reviewers have bought unquestioningly into the notion that the original Bone Suckin' Sauce was modeled on a western North Carolina–style barbecue sauce. In actuality, there really is no such sauce with any sort of traceable North Carolina tradition in that part of the state; it's simply backwash from Tennessee and points west.

A comment from a reviewer in *Country Living* magazine is revealing: "Bone Suckin' Sauce [is] sweetened with the honey and molasses you'd expect from sauce makers in Raleigh, NC. Ford's Gourmet Foods' [sauce] includes horseradish, mustard and a secret spice blend."

Molasses as an expected barbecue sauce ingredient in Raleigh? That's certainly news to me. Well, no matter. This is a really good sauce, no matter how it's described or commercially positioned. Strong, creative marketing and

Bone Suckin' Sauce

fanciful reviewing shouldn't detract in the slightest from its popularity.

BONE SUCKIN' SAUCE

Ford's Gourmet Foods

1109 Agriculture Street, Suite 1

Raleigh, N.C. 27603

919-833-7647

www.bonesuckin.com

DIMPLES BBQ SAUCE

Rich and Jan Campana of Wake Forest moved here from California in 2005 and soon became heavily involved in the competition barbecue scene, although not the traditional sector that revolves around pit cooking the whole hog. The Campanas gravitated rather toward events sanctioned by the Kansas City Barbecue Society, competing in the categories of Ribs, Chicken, Beef Brisket, and Pork. (As a sign of the changing barbecue landscape in North Carolina, KCBS now sanctions the majority of barbecue cookoffs in our state.)

The Campanas started experimenting with sauce recipes, and it wasn't long before they received enough encouragement to move ahead with turning the venture into a business. They launched Dimples BBQ Sauce in 2011. In their very first year, their creation won second place in each of the Beef, Chicken, and Pork categories of the *National Barbecue News* sauce competition. It also took a first-place honor from "The Q Review" in its 2011 Best of the Best competition, being named the top mild tomato sauce. Then Dimples placed

Dimple's BBQ Sauce

first in the "Mild Tomato" category of the National Barbecue Festival's 2012 Best of the Best contest, also winning the Reserve Grand Champion accolade. This was heady stuff for the new barbecue sauce venture.

In a 2014 review, "Taste of Southern" blogger Steve Gordon wrote, "Dimples BBQ Sauce is sweet and a little tangy all at the same time. I really like that combination, and liked that it was neither runny thin, or so thick you couldn't get it to pour out of the bottle. It was silky smooth in texture."

As for the product's name, Jan Campana, who serves as president of the business, explains that both her husband, Rich, and her two sons all have chin dimples, as do her brother and father. The Campanas also think Dimples makes a good name for a pig, the animal long the center of North Carolina barbecue.

DIMPLES BBQ SAUCE

4460 New Falls of Neuse Road
Raleigh, N.C. 27614

919-555-5555
www.dimplesbbqsauce.com

R.O.'S BARBECUE SLAW/SAUCE

R.O.'s Barbecue Slaw/Sauce

Is it slaw or is it sauce? A runny slaw, maybe. In any case, the company motto boasts, "The slaw flows at R.O.'s."

Over several generations, this unique and peculiar dressing has enjoyed much wider popularity than even the sliced barbecue sandwiches and "slaw burgers" atop which it's been served since R. O. and Pearl Black opened R.O.'s Barbecue in 1946.

Pearl Black came up with the recipe and started making the barbecue slaw by hand, using a hand grater in her home kitchen. (Health inspectors don't allow such hybrid home/restaurant practices any longer, which makes opening a small restaurant or beginning any new food venture considerably more difficult than it once was.) The "orangy slaw, sauce and dip" is now made in a production facility across from the barbecue restaurant and is aggressively marketed to grocery stores and other outlets around the southwestern Pied-

mont. Depending on the season, one thousand to two thousand containers are filled and shipped daily.

In 2003, *Saveur* magazine called R.O.'s product "the savoriest slaw in the south." "Invented in 1947," it said, "this mayo-and-ketchup based concoction, with a nice pepper and ginger kick, is far more saucy and interesting than traditional coleslaw. Spread it on meats. Dip shrimp into it. Or eat it solo with a bun the way locals do."

R.O.'s has two mobile kitchens (which the company calls "rolling billboards") that travel throughout Gaston and neighboring counties to serve up sliced barbecue sandwiches and slaw burgers, thus keeping the one-of-a-kind slaw sauce squarely in the public eye. But it is best experienced at the barbecue restaurant itself, where patrons can sample it spread on a sliced 'cue sandwich, together with a longtime favorite beverage of R.O.'s patrons, a fizzy Cherry Lemon Sun Drop.

R.O.'S BARBECUE DISTRIBUTING COMPANY LLC

1315 Gaston Avenue

Gastonia, N.C. 28052

704-853-8788

www.rosbbq.com

CAROLINA TREET

Carolina Treet Cooking Barbecue Sauce, invented in Wilmington in 1953, is really a thickened version of an eastern North Carolina vinegar-pepper sauce. It is ideal for oven-roasting barbecued chicken. One of eastern North Carolina's most famous barbecue restaurants, Wilber's in Goldsboro, serves a similar (but homemade) sauce on its barbecued chicken. Vinegary and salty, yet thick enough to cling to the meat, it always gets rave reviews.

Carolina Treet was developed around the concept of preparing rotisserie-barbecued chickens for takeout from Wilmington-area grocery stores. As the new venture was envisioned, 24 chickens could be barbecued in a Rotiss-O-Mat cooker at one time, then stored in a warmer in foil-lined bags. Before long, even five cookings per day—a total of 120 birds—weren't enough to keep up with demand, especially on Sundays. For $1.39, customers could buy a whole barbecued chicken for their Sunday main dish. Customers liked

the sauce coating the chickens so much that they began to ask for quantities they could take home. The sauce empire thus established soon eclipsed the barbecued chicken concept.

In addition to its classic Cooking Barbecue Sauce, Carolina Treet now markets a thick, sweet sauce called Big Moe's, as well as a South Carolina–style mustard sauce.

Reviewers have generally agreed that Carolina Treet's formula goes best with chicken, with pork coming in a close second. I have discovered that Carolina Treet is admirably suited for slow-roasting venison tenderloin slices. I simply place third-of-an-inch slices of tenderloin evenly over the bottom of a Pyrex baking dish, salt and pepper the meat lightly, and pour a generous amount of Carolina Treet over the venison, spreading it out with a rubber spatula. I cover the meat with foil and bake it for a couple of hours at 350 degrees until fork-tender. The vinegar and spices in Carolina Treet eliminate any hint of gaminess, and the sauce creates savory gravy that goes extremely well with rice or egg noodles.

CAROLINA TREET, INC.

P.O. Box 1017

Wilmington, N.C. 28403

910-762-1950

www.carolinatreet.com

HOT AND SEASONING SAUCES

TEXAS PETE

Winston-Salem's homegrown hot-sauce empire, Texas Pete, grew out of a decision regarding the economic survival of the Garner family (no relation).

In 1929, Thad Garner, the second-oldest son of patriarch Sam Garner, decided to use money that would otherwise have gone to his college education to buy a barbecue stand in Winston-Salem, the Dixie Pig. Along with the restaurant, the purchaser got the secret recipe for a particularly delicious barbecue sauce. While the restaurant did not survive, Garner's Barbecue Sauce was a big local hit. It wasn't long before the entire family pitched in to help make the sauce in its kitchen and sell it across North Carolina to sustain it during the Great Depression.

Sam Garner and sons Thad, Ralph, and Harold landed a contract to produce their

barbecue sauce for the armed services during World War II. They formed a partnership, built their first factory at the family homesite in northwest Winston-Salem, and incorporated the T. W. Garner Food Company—as it is still known today—in 1946.

Over the years, restaurant and barbecue sauce customers asked for a red pepper sauce as well, so the family created a new recipe. Sam Garner and his sons began to ponder a brand name for the product. To connote the spicy flavor of foods from south of the border, a marketing adviser suggested the appellation *Mexican Joe*. But Sam Garner, adamant that the new condiment have an American name, suggested that *Texas* might evoke a similar zesty, peppery image. Glancing at his son Harold, also known as Pete, the elder Garner suddenly envisioned not only the name for the hot sauce—Texas Pete—but also the likeness of a cowboy, the very symbol of rugged independence and self-reliance. Considering the popularity of movie cowboys of the time, including Tom Mix and Hopalong Cassidy, what better image for a family business fighting to survive tough times?

Over the decades, the T. W. Garner Food Company has vastly increased its Texas Pete–branded product line and has expanded its factory more times than anyone with the firm can remember. Today, in addition to the original hot sauce, the company markets a "hotter" hot sauce, a garlic-flavored hot sauce, a chipotle (smoked jalapeño) hot sauce, a pepper-vinegar sauce, three different wing sauces (Fiery Sweet, Buffalo, and Extra Mild Buffalo), hot dog chili sauce, honey mustard sauce, sea-

food cocktail sauce, and an Asian-influenced Sriracha sauce called Cha!

The reputation of the original Texas Pete, which some call the South's number-one hot sauce, is built on the principle that the heat of a sauce should never overwhelm the flavor. Die-hard fans enthuse that the sauce, made from specially grown, select red cayenne peppers, "has just the right blend of spices—not too hot, not too mild." Most users think it's ideal for every type of food, breakfast through dinner. Indeed, a TV commercial entitled "Memories" shows Texas Pete being shaken onto a variety of foods at a family cookout by children and adults alike. The spot's tag line— "This is my family and these are my memories"—seems to bespeak protection from extremes of "the spice of life," if you will.

TEXAS PETE

T. W. Garner Food Company

4045 Indiana Avenue

Winston-Salem, N.C. 27105

336-661-1550

www.texaspete.com

CACKALACKY SPICE SAUCE

It seems most commercial sauces have a story of how their creators started out in their home kitchens. If you think about it, where else would someone play around with creating a sauce? Nearly anyone would start with a pot and a stove, rather than, say, a memo pad. But once a sauce has been successfully created

Cackalacky Spice Sauce

and marketed, a narrative about starting out in a "tiny cottage kitchen"—located in Chapel Hill, in this case—provides some sparkle to the company history.

This undoubtedly helps explain the story of Cackalacky Spice Sauce, named for the way some uneducated residents used to pronounce the name of our humble state.

The mission, as described by Cackalacky creator Page Shelton, was to come up with a spiced condiment to "make bland and ordinary food taste better," which is not only a tall order but also backward from the goal you might expect—say, to come up with a great-tasting, exciting sauce to enhance one's favorite foods. But whatever works.

Most people's minds also might not turn to the sweet potato as a prime ingredient in a sauce designed to overcome blandness in food. But then the sweet potato is one of North Cackalacky's leading crops—we lead the United States in production of the tuber—so there was a natural talking point that proved hard to resist. Other ingredients include vinegar, crushed tomatoes, wine, onions, molasses, Key lime juice, brown sugar, and garlic. So it seems the sweet potatoes are there mostly to provide a story line, color, and bits of texture, rather than a dominant flavor.

Those who love this sauce really love it. One online reviewer said she uses it for everything from dipping wings and fries to adding it to mayo for a burger topping. "The whole family freaks out when the bottle gets low in the refrigerator," she wrote. "We never run out because my kids will stick the (almost) empty bottle in my purse with a post-it reading 're-place me.'"

Another fan wrote, "I sensed the mild heat right after tasting the vinegar, onions and garlic. All spices in this sauce are balanced and are employed in the right amounts." The review continued, "I placed some of the sauce on a steak. This was fantastic! It truly complemented the steak and brought out its full flavor."

On the other side of the coin, one Cackalacky taster's first reaction in a YouTube video review was, "Man, that's weird!" He went on to say unenthusiastically that the sauce "smelled like a bunch of spices" and concluded, "I'm not a fan."

Most people, though, seem to agree that Cackalacky has a winsome balance of heat, flavor, and "mouth feel." I personally find that its particular blend of spices and vegetables make it a surprisingly good condiment to add interest to a serving of eastern North Carolina chopped pork barbecue. That alone makes it worthwhile!

Cackalacky has also come out with a sweet sauce flavored with Cheerwine.

CACKALACKY, INC.

P.O. Box 4901
Chapel Hill, N.C. 27515
www.cackalacky.com

BOAR AND CASTLE SAUCE

Boar and Castle Sauce was a staple of the drive-in restaurant of the same name located at Walker Avenue and West Market Street in Greensboro from 1930 to 1980. The popular teenage hangout and cruising hub was named for a pub in a novel. If dating couples planned to smooch, they parked on the dark side of the drive-in, according to longstanding tradition.

Founder Leon Thomas used his mother's recipe to re-create a sauce with which customers at "the Castle" anointed everything from "butter steak" sandwiches to burgers to fries to onion rings. Now described as an "anything and everything sauce" and available online and in certain grocery stores, Boar and Castle Sauce was originally served warm in little cups by the restaurant's white-coated carhops. Boar and Castle Sauce is today advertised as ideal for "marinating, grilling and cooking beef, chicken, pork, veggies, fries and seafood."

The restaurant served its signature sauce only on the premises until the 1950s, when it began bottling the condiment, obtaining a federal trademark for it in 1960. After the drive-in closed in 1980, Jim Ennis, a former Boar and Castle manager, continued producing the sauce until 2008. Bottling ceased from 2008 until 2010, at which time a former regular customer obtained a license from the family of Leon Thomas and began producing the sauce once again.

This is where it gets confusing. In 2008, during the time when production of Boar and Castle Sauce had ceased, another Greensboro sauce company with the name Thomas (but with no relation to the restaurant's founder) began producing a competing condiment called Castle Sauce. Both Boar and Castle Sauce and Castle Sauce are orange in color.

At a popular former drive-in restaurant in Greensboro, Boar and Castle Sauce was served on just about everything.
CAROL W. MARTIN/
GREENSBORO HISTORICAL MUSEUM COLLECTION

Both bottles feature labels with castles and blue Old English lettering. Boar and Castle's label recommends using the sauce on burgers, fries, and steak, while the website for Castle Sauce promotes the condiment as a dressing for hamburgers, steak sandwiches, and hot dogs. Dwight Thomas, manufacturer of Castle Sauce, founded his company in 1992 and produces a wide line of condiments, among them the firm's best seller, Thomas Sauce.

Boar and Castle Sauce and Castle Sauce were both available at last report. A trademark infringement lawsuit filed in 2013 by the owners of Boar and Castle Sauce has apparently not affected the marketing of the dueling condiments. Bottles at twenty paces . . .

BOAR AND CASTLE SAUCE

North Carolina Foods, Inc.
Greensboro, N.C. 27410
336-312-8808
www.boarandcastlesauce.com

CAPSICANA ZING GOURMET SAUCE

Cheng and Weng Ng of Mebane, the inventors of Capsicana Zing Gourmet Sauce, say this sauce is a result of their romance with the red pepper. But Zing isn't a hot sauce, since its vinegar, raisins, sugar, and garlic balance out the vine-ripened red peppers to produce a big, tangy flavor that has just enough heat to be interesting—but not too much. BlowingSmokeBBQ.com explained, "Capsicana Zing has just the right touch of hot peppers to make it spicy, but not fiery hot."

The founders of Home Industries, Inc., manufacturers of Zing, grew up in Malaya, Malaysia, where they were accustomed to peppers being used on various dishes with varying levels of heat. When they emigrated to the southeastern United States decades ago, they noticed what they considered a limited range of forgettable sauces in the preparation and presentation of seafood such as shrimp. So they decided to do something about it and develop a sauce of their own. But they adapted their condiment to American tastes, coming

Capsicana Zing Gourmet Sauce is a "mature blending of East and West". It contains peppers but mutes the heat with sweet raisins and spices.
HOME INDUSTRIES

up with a "mature blending of East and West" suitable for everything from barbecued pork (of course) to dips, and from seafood to salad. (Zing also makes a doggone good Asian salad dressing.) The all-natural sauce, containing no artificial preservatives or additives, does not require refrigeration. Zing has a shelf life of thirty months, according to the Ngs.

"Splash some Zing on beef, pork, poultry, seafood and vegetables. Use it as a marinade when grilling, roasting or broiling meats. Add it to stir-fry dishes for a zesty new taste." This is the advice of Anything4Restaurants.com.

One regular customer said, "My cupboard without Zing sauce is bare, and I just can't keep house without it." Another enthusiast called the sauce "a most scrumptious and delectable adornment for ordinary food."

CAPSICANA ZING GOURMET SAUCE

Home Industries, Inc.

2538 U.S. 70

Mebane, N.C. 27302

919-563-1128

www.gourmetzingsauce.com

SNYDER'S-LANCE

WHO HASN'T ENJOYED Toast Chee crackers or a bag of pretzels by Snyder's of Hanover? The names are synonymous with snacks across the whole country.

Lance was created in 1913 by food broker Philip L. Lance of Charlotte after he got stuck with five hundred pounds of unwanted raw peanuts. Instead of reneging on his deal, he was inspired to roast and sell the nuts in nickel bags. When the venture was immediately successful, Lance expanded into peanut butter. By 1915, his son-in-law, Salem Van Every, was a partner. And thus was born the concept of peanut butter spread between two crackers.

Lance grew and prospered through the Great Depression, first distributing its classic Toast Chee crackers in 1928. After expanding its product line, it replaced its honor-system coin boxes with vending machines in 1954. (In certain regions of North Carolina, in gen-

eral stores, gas stations, and even some restaurants, six-cracker Lance packages were displayed on what were commonly and generically known as "Nab racks," although the name was based on a competing brand name, Nabisco. Many rural and small-town Tar Heels routinely referred to peanut butter or cheese-spread cracker sandwiches as "Nabs," regardless of the manufacturer.) In 1982, Lance packaged its various snacks for sale in grocery stores.

Snyder's of Hanover began in 1909 when Pennsylvanian Harry Warehime founded the Hanover Pretzel Company, believing everyone would love his recipe for the crunchy, salty curlicues. The merger of Snyder's of Hanover and Lance in 2010 created the second-largest salty snack maker in the United States. The company has been a leader in creating healthier snack options and has continually expanded its product line.

Lance cracker sandwiches feature an assortment of cheese and peanut butter fillings.

LANCE, INC.

8600 South Boulevard

Charlotte, N.C. 28273

704-554-1421

www.lance.com

SNYDER'S-LANCE, INC.

P.O. Box 6917

Hanover, Pa. 17331

800-233-7125

www.snydersofhanover.com

IMAGINE A SWELTERING summer afternoon in 1950s North Carolina. You pull into a gas station or a small market, make a beeline to the cold-drink case, put your face down in the cooler, and pull out a perfectly chilled soft drink—no "sodas" in the North Carolina lexicon of that era! Chances are good the frosty drink would have been a homegrown Pepsi or Cheerwine. Just a few years later, it might have been a Sun Drop.

PEPSI

Call it Pepsi or Pepsi-Cola, this iconic soft drink is a beloved international product that originated in New Bern. Caleb Bradham introduced Brad's Drink, as it was first named, in 1898. He made and sold it at his downtown drugstore, his modest goals being to establish an appealing aid to digestion, to boost customers' energy, and to make his pharmacy/soda fountain a local gathering spot. He renamed it Pepsi-Cola for two of its principal ingredients, pepsin and kola nuts, applying for a trademark for the Pepsi-Cola name in 1902.

Pepsi's first of many advertising campaigns crowed that the drink was "exhilarating, invigorating, aids digestion." That was in 1903, by which time Pepsi-Cola had been officially registered with the United States Patent Office. Bradham sold 7,968 gallons of syrup and began issuing bottling franchises to private investors.

The company's early growth was spectacular. In 1909, Bradham built a New Bern

headquarters so lavish it was pictured on a postcard printed by the town. Unfortunately, things didn't continue to go swimmingly. World War I increased the cost of doing business, as sugar prices moved between record highs and lows. Bradham had to speculate on the sugar market to survive. Bankrupt by 1921, he was forced to sell the company.

After several owners came and went, Pepsi-Cola was acquired by Charles G. Guth, president of Loft Inc., a large chain of candy stores and soda fountains along the East Coast. Wanting to discontinue his unsatisfactory relationship with Coca-Cola, Guth returned Pepsi-Cola to its previously lofty position as a successful national brand. Caleb Bradham, meanwhile, labored quietly in his drugstore for the rest of his working life.

The original store/soda fountain has now been turned into the Birthplace of Pepsi, a popular tourist stop within easy walking distance of the town marina in New Bern. Meanwhile, the PepsiCo conglomerate is headquartered in Purchase, New York.

BIRTHPLACE OF PEPSI

256 Middle Street
New Bern, N.C. 28560
252-636-5898
www.pepsistore.com
Open daily

A vintage Pepsi poster
UNC-TV

CHEERWINE

Created in 1917 in Salisbury by general-store owner L. D. Peeler, this singular soft drink with a hint of wild cherry and a bubbly effervescence became an immediate hit. Folks from all around the county came to Peeler's store to sample the carbonated fountain drink he created using an interesting cherry-flavored concentrate he had purchased from a St. Louis–based traveling salesman. Soon, cold-drink cases all over North Carolina were filled with the "Nectar of North Carolina," said to put a smile on the lips of everyone who gave it a try. What is now marketed as "the Legend" was born.

Only a year or so after the drink's invention, a Rowan County father reportedly took the trouble and expense of sending two carefully wrapped bottles of Cheerwine to his son in wartime Europe. The bottles were included in an armed services package delivered to the son's World War I foxhole. The son and his fellow combatants are said to have left the two empty bottles upended on sticks rammed into the foxhole's earth floor, marking the location of a couple of "dead soldiers," as it were.

President Dwight Eisenhower visited Salisbury in 1953 to celebrate the two hundredth anniversary of Rowan County. There, he became the first president to drink a Cheerwine. It is rumored that he proclaimed, "Ike likes!"

Generations later, some say Cheerwine has grown larger than life. Customers in every state in the country are mildly addicted to the concoction, and Cheerwine is regularly spotted at places such as the Great Wall of

At one point, bottles of Cheerwine were filled manually.
CHEERWINE

China, the fjords of northern Europe, and the battlefields of Iraq.

CHEERWINE

Carolina Beverage Corporation

1413 Jake Alexander Boulevard South

Salisbury, N.C. 28146

704-637-5881

www.cheerwine.com

SUN DROP

Many people consider Sun Drop the ultimate citrusy thirst-quenching drink.

Like many drinks, Sun Drop began as a recipe scribbled on paper—in this case by Charles Lazier in 1928, as he was riding around St. Louis, Missouri. It was patented on April 15, 1930. In 1953, a soft-drink bottler

An old Sun Drop bottle

in Gaston County, Charles P. Nanney, became the first Sun Drop bottler in the country. He had met Lazier at a national bottling show, where Lazier gave the North Carolinian a sample of his invention. After working to improve Lazier's formula to create the taste he wanted, Nanney started exploring ways to market his new version of the drink.

He eventually teamed up with an old friend, Red Bridges, owner of Bridges Barbecue Lodge in Shelby, who was opening his now-famous restaurant on U.S. 74 Bypass. The pair gave away free samples of barbecue and seven-ounce glasses of Sun Drop. The original slogan boasted, "Refreshing as a cup of coffee"—and indeed, the drink has as least as much caffeine as coffee. Sun Drop was an immediate success.

During the 1980s and early 1990s, Sun Drop was promoted by NASCAR driver and native North Carolinian Dale Earnhardt. National distribution of the drink began in 2011. It is now part of Dr Pepper/Snapple, headquartered in Texas.

DR PEPPER/
SNAPPLE GROUP, INC.

5301 Legacy Drive

Plano, Tex. 75024

800-696-5891

www.drpeppersnapplegroup.com

INDEX